Migration and Environmental Change in the West African Sahel

T0298385

The West African Sahel is predicted to be heavily affected by climate change in the future. Slow-onset environmental changes, such as increasing rainfall variability and rising temperature, are presumed to worsen the livelihood conditions and to increase the out-migration from the affected regions.

Based on qualitative and quantitative data from study areas in Mali and Senegal, this book examines the relationship between population dynamics, livelihoods and environment in the Sahel region, focussing specifically on motives for migration. Critiquing the assumption that environmental stress is the dominating migration driver, the author demonstrates the important role of individual aspirations and social processes, such as educational opportunities and the pull of urban lifestyles. In doing so, the book provides a more nuanced picture of the environment-migration nexus, arguing that slow-onset environmental changes may actually be less important as drivers of migration in the Sahel than they are often depicted in the media and climate change literature.

This is a valuable resource for academics and students of environmental sociology, migration and development studies.

Victoria van der Land is a sociologist with a research focus on climate change and migration. She has extensive work and field experience in West African countries, such as Benin, Chad, Cote d'Ivoire, Mali and Senegal. Currently, she works as a DAAD lecturer at the University of Bamako, Mali.

Routledge Studies in Environmental Migration, Displacement and Resettlement

Migration and Environmental Change in the West African Sahel

Why Capabilities and Aspirations Matter

Victoria van der Land

Routledge
Taylor & Francis Group
LONDON AND NEW YORK

earthscan
from Routledge

First published 2018 by Routledge

2 Park Square, Milton Park, Abingdon, Oxfordshire OX14 4RN
52 Vanderbilt Avenue, New York, NY 10017

Routledge is an imprint of the Taylor & Francis Group, an informa business

First issued in paperback 2019

British Library Cataloguing-in-Publication Data
A catalogue record for this book is available from the British Library

Library of Congress Cataloging-in-Publication Data
A catalog record for this book has been requested

ISBN: 978-1-138-21752-2 (hbk)
ISBN: 978-0-367-24952-6 (pbk)

Typeset in Goudy
by Apex CoVantage, LLC

Contents

Figures

Tables

Boxes

Abbreviations

ANSD	*Agence National de la Statistique et de la Démographie, Senegal*
BMBF	*Bundesministerium für Bildung und Forschung; German Federal Ministry of Education and Research*
CA	*Capability Approach*
CIESIN	*Center for International Earth Science Information Network, Columbia University, New York*
ECOWAS	*Economic Community of West African States*
EU	*European Union*
FDI	*Foreign Direct Investment*
GPCC	*Global Precipitation Climatology Centre*
INSTAT	*Institut National de la Statistique du Mali*
IOM	*International Organization for Migration*
IPCC	*Intergovernmental Panel on Climate Change*
ISOE	*Institut für sozial-ökologische Forschung, Institute for Social-Ecological Research*
LARTES/IFAN	*Le Laboratoire de Recherche sur les Transformations Economiques et Sociales/Institut Fondamental d'Afrique Noir*
NGO	*Non-Governmental Organization*
ODA	*Official Development Assistance*
SLA	*Sustainable Livelihoods Approach*
TRMM	*Tropical Rainfall Measuring Mission*
UN	*United Nations*
UNDP	*United Nations Development Programme*
UNEP	*United Nations Environment Programme*
UNHCR	*United Nations High Commissioner for Refugees*

Acknowledgements

The present book includes research conducted within the micle project on migration, climate change and environment, which was funded by the German Federal Ministry of Education and Research (BMBF), grant number 01UV1007A (see www.micle-project.net).

The author owes particular thanks to Diana Hummel (Institute for Social-Ecological Research – ISOE) and Uta Ruppert (Goethe University Frankfurt) for supervising and supporting the doctoral thesis on which this book is based.

Special thanks goes to the micle project team for the fruitful collaboration, including Martin Doevenspeck, Cyrus Samimi, Clemens Romankiewicz, Martin Brandt, Lukas Drees, Stefan Liehr, Julia Röhrig, Diana Kaiser, Wolfgang Lutz and Samir KC, as well as to Nadia Anoumou, Anais Fournier, Joel Fourier and Kristine Albrektsen.

The author is particularly grateful for the support of the Institute for Social-Ecological Research (ISOE) in Frankfurt, Germany and the valuable comments of Susana Adamo and colleagues from the Center for International Earth Science Information Network (CIESIN) at Columbia University, New York, as well as of Sally Findley, Sabine Henry and Haydea Izazola on parts of the thesis that helped develop the ideas of the book. The author also thanks the anonymous reviewers for the valuable comments and Mihoko Fujioka for commenting, Elnaz Rashidian for the map and Trang Nguyen for proofreading.

The book would not have been possible without the tremendous support of many people in Mali and Senegal. Special thanks go to LARTES/IFAN, University Cheikh Anta Diop of Dakar, Senegal, particularly Abdou S. Fall, and Point Sud in Bamako, Mali, for the excellent cooperation. The author also thanks the translators, particularly Oumar Sow and Yaya Koétiumbé for their support. The author is most grateful to the interviewees without whom this book would not have been realised.

Last, but not least, the author would like to thank friends and family for their constant support as well as Jan Schumacher for his advice and encouragement.

1 Introduction

Climate change, environment and migration

The impact of climate change on population mobility as a popular topic

Today, images and headlines of African migrants desperately trying to enter Europe fill the media news and shape the public opinion on migration from Africa to Europe. The media takes up images of migrants undertaking dangerous journeys by crossing the sea in overcrowded boats from Northern and Western Africa to Europe and of desperate migrants storming the fences of the Spanish exclaves of Ceuta and Melilla in North Africa. In addition, the political and public debates on global warming and climate change emphasise their urgency with images of disaster-hit landscapes and suffering people. Due to these images, the Sahel region became synonymous with drought-hit soils and starving people during severe droughts.

The impact of climate change on human mobility moved into the centre of interest and concern in the mid-1980s, when the term *environmental refugee* was brought into public by a United Nations Environment Programme (UNEP) publication (El-Hinnawi 1985). At about the same time, climate change entered the public debate with the First Assessment Report of the Intergovernmental Panel on Climate Change (IPCC) and presumed that climate change could strongly affect human migration (IPCC 1990). Predictions of tens or even hundreds of millions of environmental refugees as a consequence of climate change boosted this interest in the 1990s (Jacobson 1988; Myers and Kent 1995). Later, a few reports even argued for a potential mass migration as a result of climate change and increased the estimated number of people affected by climate change to up to 1 billion by 2050 (Christian Aid 2007).

Although these numbers have been criticised as highly speculative, they have been cited even years later – often being treated as empirical evidence – and have had a major impact on politics, media and academia (Brown 2008b; Gemenne 2011). The high number of potential environmental refugees and the alarmist rhetoric concerning climate change and its impact on humanity expressed by various actors, including UN agencies, non-governmental organisations (NGOs), national governments and popular media, sparked political debate and interest in the topic. It also raised concerns that they may threaten national and international security in the "global North" (Homer-Dixon 1991; Kibreab 1997).

During the last two decades, there has been an enormous increase of case studies and several research projects on the linkages between population movements and climate change in particular – and environmental change in a more general manner (Laczko and Piguet 2014). The studies cover regions all over the world, including developed and developing countries, and focus on various environmental phenomena. One-third of the existing research studies and publications on environment and migration focuses on Africa with the Sahel region used as a prominent example of migration caused by drought and/or rainfall variability. The West African Sahel is presumed to be one of the regions that will be most affected by climate and environmental change in the future and the impact of environmental changes on human populations in the region is a major global concern (Dilley et al. 2005; IPCC 2007).

The development of the environment-migration research

The increasing interest on the linkages between climate change and mobility and differing academic perspectives of the term *environmental refugees* led to fundamental research and developments on the subject. The development in research in turn influenced the political debate and public opinion on the effects of climate change on human mobility. In academia, a disciplinary divide between natural scientists and social scientists marked the discourse on the linkages between climate change, environment and migration, pushing the research forward. The proponents of the term *environmental refugees* were usually natural scientists also referred to as "environmentalists." They supported the concept of *environmental refugees* aimed at directing public attention to the negative human impacts of environmental changes. The critics of the term were often migration scholars who criticised and challenged the concept of *environmental refugees* (Suhrke 1994; Kibreab 1997; Castles 2011; Morrissey 2012b).

Critical research of the term *environmental refugees* started dominating the view on the linkages between environmental change and migration in academia in the early 2000s and led to important changes in research. The research on the linkages of climate change and migration henceforward distinguished between slow-onset environmental changes and rapid-onset changes. Research on migration and slow-onset environmental changes shifted towards a more positive and proactive understanding of the people and their mobility in the context of environmental change. Table 1.1 illustrates the different shifts included in the development of the research on the linkages between slow-environmental changes and migration.

Earlier research assumed a mono-causal relationship between the environment and population displacement by considering environmental degradation and global warming as a direct cause of potential large-scale population displacements. In contrast, migration scholars argued that migration is multi-causal and that environmental factors are not the only and often not the predominant cause of migration. Today, academics and non-academics commonly agree that migration in the context of slow-onset environmental changes is multi-causal; environmental

Table 1.1 Shifts towards a positive understanding of people and mobility in the context of environmental changes.

	Earlier view		*Current view*
Link between environment and mobility	mono-causal	➜	multi-causal
Mobility as	failure to adapt to change	➜	adaptation strategy
Character of mobility	forced	➜	voluntary
People considered as	victims of global warming	➜	agents adapting to change
Term used	environmental refugees	➜	environmental migrants

Source: Author.

factors almost always interact with other cultural, demographic, economic, political and social drivers of migration (Piguet et al. 2011; Hummel et al. 2012; Laczko and Piguet 2014; McLeman 2014). The mono-causal approach assumed that environmental degradation leads to migration. Therefore, the predicted numbers of environmental refugees were often based on the number of people living in areas identified to be prone to the effects of global warming. Migration scholars criticised that being at risk does not necessarily directly result in displacement or migration, but that coping strategies and adaptive practices and the local context have to be considered (Lonergan 1998; Black 2001; Castles 2002). By considering migration as one possible coping strategy, the perspective of migration changed from a passive towards a more positive and a proactive view on mobility.

At the same time people's vulnerability became the crucial link between the environment and the migration decision and their available strategies to cope with or adapt to environmental stress emerged as a key focus for research (Kelly and Adger 2000; Cutter et al. 2003; Oliver-Smith and Shen 2009). Consequently, the view of mobility as a failure to adapt to environmental changes shifted to a more positive view of migration as an adaptation strategy to environmental stress. Today, research considers migration in the context of slow-onset environmental changes mainly as an adaptation strategy to diversify people's income sources and to reduce their vulnerability to external environmental and non-environmental stress (McLeman and Hunter 2010; Adger and Adams 2013; Ober 2014). With that, the view on migrants shifted from passive victims of environmental stress to a more positive perception of agents whose migration is a conscious decision in order to adapt to environmental stress.

At the same time, this also changed the perception of mobility from forced to voluntary. Nevertheless, research agrees that population movements caused by climate or environmental change range from voluntary to forced and that most migrations contain elements of both (Richmond 1993; Morrissey 2012a). While earlier studies on migrants considered them the most vulnerable to environmental stress, recent literature regards those who are not able to migrate as the most vulnerable. These people have been labelled as "trapped populations" (Adger et al. 2014; Black and Collyer 2014).

As a consequence of this general shift in the environment-migration research the controversial term *environmental refugees* was replaced little by little by the term *environmental migrants*. Migration scholars and refugee specialists rejected the term *environmental refugee* due to the legal and political implications linked to the term *refugee* (Brown 2008a; Afifi and Jäger 2010). The legal definition of refugees only includes people who have crossed international borders to seek protection from political persecution. People affected by environmental changes rather move within their country. In contrast, the term *migrant* reflects the agency of the people, acknowledges the potential voluntary characteristic and highlights the multi-causality of the movement. Up to now, there is no consensus on a common definition of an appropriate term or concept. International Organization for Migration (IOM) offers an often cited working definition as follows:

> **Environmental migrants** are persons or groups of persons who, for compelling reasons of sudden or progressive changes in the environment that adversely affect their lives or living conditions, are obliged to leave their habitual homes, or choose to do so, either temporarily or permanently, and who move either within their country or abroad.
>
> (IOM 2007: 1)

The continuous advancement of environment-migration research in academics had a ripple effect on the political debate on climate change and the impact of human mobility. Eventually also governments, international agencies, non-governmental organisations, the media, and civil society adapted the critical perspective of migration scholars and considered the role of migration as an adaptation strategy to maintain livelihoods in response to environmental changes.

Challenges and consensus within the environment-migration nexus

Despite progress in the environment-migration research and the increasing number of publications, the effects of environmental or climate change on human mobility remain unclear. The results are often highly context-specific and difficult to generalise. Even case studies that focus on the same wider region vary in focus, methods, concepts and theories, if any, and are therefore difficult to compare (Jónsson 2010; van der Land *et al.* forthcoming). General difficulties for comparing case studies result from a lack of definitions for *environmental migrants* or terms such as *migration* and *climate change* or *environmental change*. Studies often refer to different factors, such as changes in the environment (e.g. land degradation, changes in rainfall, temperature or vegetation) or types of migration (e.g. only first migration, migration intention or life history of migrations) and use different spatial scales, ranging from a village to several countries in one geographical region. In addition to the multiple factors that influence human mobility, in many areas – and particularly in the Sahel – people have been mobile and have been living with highly variable climatic conditions for generations. The establishment of migration in society makes it even more difficult to identify net effects of environmental changes (Black *et al.* 2011).

Against the backdrop of these difficulties, it is not surprising that many studies often only come to vague results and minimal agreement on the complexity and context-dependency of migration. Concrete conclusions on the environment-migration nexus are rare and the linkages remain unclear. Examples for such conclusions include "the impacts are difficult to predict" (Meze-Hausken 2000: 401) or "environmental stress can play an important role in the migration decision, but the relationship is complex" (Morrissey 2012a: 142). This is unsatisfying and does not contribute much to advance the knowledge on the impact of environmental change on migration. It remains unclear to what extent climate and environmental change may exacerbate socio-economic problems and which effects they will have on migration in the future. Nevertheless, the research community has at least widely agreed on the following conclusions about the environment-migration nexus (e.g. Schmidt-Verkerk 2011; Bremner and Hunter 2014; Laczko and Piguet 2014):

- Migration is complex and multi-causal. In most cases, it depends on many other factors besides the environment.
- The local context is crucial because it influences the causes of migration and alternative local strategies available to cope with environmental stress.
- People usually can choose among a variety of strategies, migration being one, to cope with environmental stress, which implies that environmental change does not necessarily lead to migration.
- Most migrations from areas affected by environmental change are considered a preventative and voluntary household livelihood or adaptation strategy.
- Migrations from areas affected by environmental change are mostly short-distance and short-term moves.
- Individual characteristics, such as age, gender, marital status and education, can have a considerable effect on people's vulnerability to environmental stress and the decision to migrate.
- The predictions of a high number of displaced people have been oversimplified and are unlikely to become reality.

This book's contribution

This book aims to contribute to a better understanding of the relationship between population mobility, livelihoods and the environment in the West African Sahel. The impact of environmental changes on human populations in the West African Sahel is a major global concern and has attracted considerable research interest over the past decades. However, the impact of environmental change on mobility now and in the future remains unclear. The environment-migration research includes different dimension (see e.g. Adamo 2009), but this book elaborates only on slow-onset environmental changes, such as changes in rainfall and land degradation, as a potential cause of migration in the West

African Sahel. In contrast to sudden natural disasters whereby the impact of geophysical factors is immediately evident, the role of environmental factors on human mobility is less clear and difficult to measure in the case of slow-onset environmental changes.

The present book is based on a dissertation (van der Land 2015) that has been part of the interdisciplinary research project "micle – Migration, climate change and environment: social-ecological conditions of population movements in the Sahelian countries Mali and Senegal" funded by the German Federal Ministry of Education and Research (BMBF). For more information, see www.micle-project.net.

In order to contribute to a better understanding of the impact of environmental factors on population mobility, this book builds on qualitative and quantitative empirical research conducted in two rural study areas: in Bandiagara in Mali and Linguère in Senegal. For the analysis, it pursues a different approach to most case studies conducted in the region. For a detailed overview on already existing case study on the environment-migration nexus in Sub-Saharan Africa, see e.g. Jónsson 2010; Morrissey 2014; van der Land et al. forthcoming. The approach in this book first focuses on individuals and their migration decision rather than on households. With its focus on individuals, the book considers the migrants' sorrows and desires and contrasts them with the prevailing research view that depicts migration mostly as a household adaptation strategy in response to environmental change. Second, it analyses people's reasons to stay and to migrate in a more comprehensive manner in order to identify the role of environmental reasons to migrate relative to other migration reasons and motives. Third, it examines people's capabilities to decide between migrating and staying and their preferences and aspirations for one or the other, in order to understand why some people migrate and others stay in areas affected by environmental change.

This book builds on the view of migration scholars who advocated the multi-causality of migration in the environment-migration nexus and combines a development approach with a social-ecological perspective to analyse the environment-migration nexus. It starts from the premise that natural and social processes are highly intertwined and dependent on each other and thus cannot be examined separately (Becker and Jahn 2006; Hummel *et al.* 2011). It uses the term *social* in a broader sense, including cultural, demographic, economic and political aspects. Further, it highlights the relevance of development with respect to the linkages between environmental change and migration in different ways. It adapts the view of livelihood research which considers migration not only as a coping strategy for external stress but also a means to increase financial resources and development. Inspired by Amartya Sen's Capability Approach, it also highlights the role of development for widening choices and capabilities with respect to the migration decision. A lack of development can generate vulnerabilities to environmental change that in turn can exacerbate difficult living conditions and aggravate already existing problems such as poverty and inequality, thereby resulting in potential migration (Lonergan 1998;

Black 2001; Castles 2002). In contrast, development encourages migration, even from areas affected by environmental change, and shapes the migration decision of individuals and households in a positive or negative way. The book argues that development and social transformation processes, like an increasing level of education and/or changes in lifestyle and traditional norms, may reduce the impact of environmental stress on people's livelihoods and migration, despite worsening climate conditions.

As a conceptual contribution to the environment-migration research, the book provides a new approach based on two development theories: the Sustainable Livelihood Approach and Sen's Capability Approach. This *Capability and Aspirations Approach* aims for a better understanding of the linkages between the environment and migration in general and for the West African Sahel in particular. In order to achieve this aim, it considers people's capabilities to migrate, their individual aspirations and migration motives – in addition to the household's needs – as well as social transformation processes. This comprehensive view is important to be able to assess the consequences of environmental change for migration and to act or implement efficient measures promptly in order to avoid natural hazards turning into disasters.

Book outline

The chapters follow an order that build on one another. It is, however, also possible for readers interested only in one or several particular chapters to read them independently from each other.

Chapter 2 starts with an introduction to the two rural study areas: Bandiagara in Mali and Linguère in Senegal, and briefly explains the research methods. It includes the climatic and environmental stressors, livelihood conditions and migration patterns in the two rural areas.

Chapter 3 presents the *Capability and Aspirations Approach* based on the Sustainable Livelihoods Approach and Amartya Sen's Capability Approach, as new theoretical framework for the research on the environment-migration nexus.

Chapter 4 illustrates the variety of people's migration motives, often dependent on individual characteristics and the different role of environmental factors in the migration decision among people in both study areas.

Chapter 5 explains that migration is, in many cases, not a household decision and demonstrates that people have different capabilities to choose between migrating and staying.

Chapter 6 shows that preference and aspirations shape the migration decision and that young people often aspire to a life without agriculture.

Chapter 7 argues that development and social transformation processes, like an increasing level of education and urbanisation, may reduce the impact of environmental stress on people's livelihoods and migration.

Chapter 8 offers a migrant typology that describes seven types of migrants by differing characteristics and the impact of environmental factors on their migration.

Chapter 9 illustrates the different notions of migration in the "global North" and "South" and explains why migration motives carry more similarities than perceived.

Chapter 10 concludes the main findings of the book and gives some recommendations for policy makers, as well as avenues for further research.

Bibliography

Adamo, S.B. 2009 "Environmentally induced population displacements", in IHDP Secretariat ed. *Social challenges of change.* (IHDP update, *Magazine of the International Human Dimensions Programme on Global Environmental Change*), Bonn, 13–21.

Adger, N. and Adams, H. 2013 "Migration as an adaptation strategy to environmental change", in ISSC/UNESCO eds. *World social science report 2013: Changing global environments*, International Social Science Council (ISSC); United Nations Educational, Scientific and Cultural Organization (UNESCO), Paris: OECD Publishing and UNESCO Publishing, 261–264.

Adger, W.N., Pulhin, J.M., Barnett, J., Dabelko, G.D., Hovelsrud, G.K., Levy, M., Oswald Spring, Ú. and Vogel, C.H. 2014 "Human security", in *Climate change 2014: Impacts, adaptation, and vulnerability. Part A: Global and sectoral aspects*, Cambridge: Cambridge University Press, 755–791.

Afifi, T. and Jäger, J. eds. 2010 *Environment, forced migration and social vulnerability*, Berlin: Springer.

Becker, E. and Jahn, T. 2006 *Soziale Ökologie: Grundzüge einer Wissenschaft von den gesellschaftlichen Naturverhältnissen*, Frankfurt am Main, New York: Campus.

Black, R. 2001 *Environmental refugees: Myth or reality?* (New Issues in Refugee Research; Working Paper 34), United Nations High Commissioner for Refugees (UNHCR).

Black, R., Adger, W.N., Arnell, N.W., Dercon, S., Geddes, A. and Thomas, D. 2011 "The effect of environmental change on human migration" *Global Environmental Change*, 21, S3–S11.

Black, R. and Collyer, M. 2014 "Populations 'trapped' at times of crisis" *Forced Migration Review*, 45, 52–56.

Bremner, J. and Hunter, L.M. 2014 "Migration and the environment" *Population Bulletin*, 69(1).

Brown, O. 2008a *Migration and climate change*, Geneva: International Organization for Migration (IOM).

Brown, O. 2008b "The numbers game" *Forced Migration Review*, 31, 8–9.

Castles, S. 2002 *Environmental change and forced migration: Making sense of the debate* (New Issues in Refugee Research, Working Paper 70), Geneva: United Nations High Commissioner for Refugees (UNHCR).

Castles, S. 2011 "Concluding remarks on the climate change-migration nexus", in Piguet, E., Pécoud, A. and Guchteneire, P.F.A. de eds. *Migration and climate change*, Cambridge: Cambridge University Press, 415–427.

Christian Aid 2007 *Human tide: The real migration crisis*. A Christian Aid report, May.

Cutter, S.L., Boruff, B.J. and Shirley, L.W. 2003 "Social vulnerability to environmental hazards" *Social Science Quarterly*, 84(2), 242–261.

Dilley, M., Chen, R.S., Deichmann, U., Lerner-Lam, A.L. and Arnold, M. 2005 *Natural disaster hotspots: A global risk analysis* (Disaster risk management series), Washington, DC: The World Bank.

El-Hinnawi, E.E. 1985 *Environmental refugees*, Nairobi: United Nations Environment Programme.

Gemenne, F. 2011 "Why the numbers don't add up: A review of estimates and predictions of people displaced by environmental changes" *Global Environmental Change*, 21, S41–S49.

Homer-Dixon, T.F. 1991 "On the threshold: Environmental changes as causes of acute conflict" *International Security*, 16(2), 76–116.

Hummel, D., Doevenspeck, M. and Samimi, C. 2012 *Climate change, environment and migration in the Sahel: Selected issues with a focus on Mali and Senegal* (micle – Working Paper 1), Frankfurt am Main: Institute for Social-Ecological Research (ISOE).

Hummel, D., Jahn, T. and Schramm, E. 2011 *Social-ecological analysis of climate induced changes in biodiversity: Outline of a research concept* (Knowledge Flow Paper 11), Frankfurt am Main: Biodiversität und Klima Forschungszentrum (BiK-F), Institute for Social-Ecological Research.

IOM 2007 *Discussion note: Migration and the environment* (Ninety-fourth Session, MC/INF/288), International Organization for Migration (IOM).

IPCC 1990 *Climate change: The IPCC impacts assessment*. Report prepared for IPCC by Working Group II, Canberra.

IPCC 2007 *Climate change 2007: The physical science basis. Contribution of working group I to the fourth assessment report of the intergovernmental panel on climate change*, Cambridge and New York: Cambridge University Press.

Jacobson, J.L. 1988 *Environmental refugees: A yardstick of habitability* (Worldwatch Paper 86), Washington, DC: Worldwatch Institute.

Jónsson, G. 2010 *The environmental factor in migration dynamics – a review of African case studies* (Working Papers 21), Oxford: International Migration Institute (IMI). James Martin 21st Century School, University of Oxford.

Kelly, M.P. and Adger, N.W. 2000 "Theory and practice in assessing vulnerability to climate change and facilitating adaptation" *Climatic Change*, 47, 325–352.

Kibreab, G. 1997 "Environmental causes and impact of refugee movements: A critique of the current debate" *Disasters*, 21(1), 20–38.

Laczko, F. and Piguet, E. 2014 "Regional perspectives on migration, the environment and climate change", in Piguet, E. and Laczko, F. eds. *People on the move in a changing climate: The regional impact of environmental change on migration* (2), Dordrecht, The Netherlands: Springer, 1–20.

Lonergan, S. 1998 "The role of environmental degradation in population displacement" *Environmental Change and Security Project Report*, 4, 5–15.

McLeman, R.A. 2014 *Climate and human migration: Past experiences, future challenges*, New York: Cambridge University Press.

McLeman, R.A. and Hunter, L.M. 2010 "Migration in the context of vulnerability and adaptation to climate change: Insights from analogues" *Wiley Interdisciplinary Reviews: Climate Change*, 1(3), 450–461.

Meze-Hausken, E. 2000 "Migration caused by climate change: How vulnerable are people inn dryland areas?" *Mitigation and Adaptation Strategies for Global Change*, 5(4), 379–406.

Morrissey, J. 2012a "Contextualizing links between migration and environmental change in northern Ethiopia", in Hastrup, K. and Fog Olwig, K. eds. *Climate change and human mobility: Global challenges to the social sciences*, Cambridge: Cambridge University Press, 110–146.

Morrissey, J. 2012b "Rethinking the 'debate on environmental refugee': From 'maximalists and minimalists' to 'proponents and critics'" *Journal of Political Ecology*, 19, 37–49.

Morrissey, J. 2014 "Environmental change and human migration in Sub-Saharan Africa", in Piguet, E. and Laczko, F. eds. *People on the move in a changing climate: The regional impact of environmental change on migration* (2), Dordrecht, The Netherlands: Springer, 81–109.

Myers, N. and Kent, J. 1995 *Environmental exodus: An emergent crisis in the global arena*, Washington, DC: Climate Inst.

Ober, K. 2014 *Migration as adaptation: Exploring mobility as a coping strategy for climate change*, Oxford: Climate Change and Migration Coalition, Climate Outreach and Information Network.

Oliver-Smith, A. and Shen, X. 2009 *Linking environmental change, migration & social vulnerability* (Source – Studies of the University: Research, Counsel, Education – Public Series of UNU-EHS 12), Bonn: United Nations University Institute for Environment and Human Security; Munich Re Foundation.

Piguet, E., Pécoud, A. and Guchteneire, P.F.A. de eds. 2011 *Migration and climate change*, Cambridge: Cambridge University Press.

Richmond, A.H. 1993 "Reactive migration: Sociological perspectives on refugee movements" *Journal of Refugee Studies*, 6(1), 7–24.

Schmidt-Verkerk, K. 2011 *The potential influence of climate change on migratory behaviour – a study of drought, hurricanes and migration in Mexico*. Dissertation. University of Sussex.

Suhrke, A. 1994 "Environmental degradation and population flows" *Journal of International Affairs*, 47(2), 473–496.

van der Land, V. 2015 *The environment-migration nexus reconsidered: why capabilities and aspirations matter*. Dissertation. Goethe-Universität Frankfurt.

van der Land, V., Romankiewicz, C. and van der Geest, K. forthcoming "Environment and migration – a review of West African case studies", in McLeman, R. and Gemenne, F. eds. *The Routledge handbook of environmental displacement and migration*, Routledge.

2 Livelihoods, environmental stress and mobility in Mali and Senegal

Climate change and human mobility in the West African Sahel

The West African Sahel is one of the poorest regions in the world and presumed to be one of the areas that will be most affected by climate and environmental change in the future. Increasing temperatures, decreasing precipitation and increasing variability of rainfall are likely to cause land degradation, desertification and droughts – consequently, affecting food production, pasture productivity and the livelihoods of the people (IPCC 2007). The Sahel is a semiarid area with an annual average precipitation between 200 and 600 mm, stretching from the West to the East of the African continent through the following countries: Senegal, Mauritania, Mali, Burkina Faso, Niger, Nigeria, Cameroon, Chad, Sudan, Eritrea and Ethiopia. Bordered by the Sahara desert in the North and the Savannah in the South, it has very few significant urban centres (OECD 2009).

During the last century, four major droughts occurred in the Sahel (1909–13, 1940–44, 1969–73 and 1983–85), leaving devastating effects on the natural environment, livestock and people (OECD 2009). In particular, the severe droughts of the 1970s and 1980s that caused a major famine, attracted a high level of interest from the international community. Over the last several decades, climate conditions have changed in the region. Rainfall variability and temperatures have increased and are likely to continue in the future. The predictions for rainfall are less clear; thus, whether the Sahel will become more or less wet in the future remains uncertain (IPCC 2007, 2013). Nevertheless, it is expected to become drier due to rising temperatures. The highly variable rainfall – including the timing, length and volume of rain within and between years – is the dominant environmental risk that farmers and livestock keepers face in the Sahel (Mortimore and Adams 1999; Sissoko et al. 2011). People's yields are highly dependent on the quantity and quality of rainfall during the three-month rainy season from July to September.

Today, the impact of climate change and climate variability on human populations, on their livelihoods and on their need to migrate, is a major concern in the West African Sahel. Migration from areas affected by environmental changes is presumed to be linked to these changes, either as a direct response to economic needs caused by poor yields or as an adaptation strategy to cope with present and future stress. People's livelihoods are highly dependent on small-scale agricultural production. In addition to environmental stress, rapid population growth places pressure on available natural resources (Hammer 2004; Mertz et al. 2011; de Sherbinin et al. 2012).

West Africa is the most mobile part of the continent. People in the Sahel, in particular, have a long tradition of population mobility that includes a multitude of migration patterns and trajectories (Cordell et al. 1996; Rain 1999; IOM 2014). Today mobility in the West African Sahel is dominated by migration within the country or to neighbouring countries. Migration is often seasonal mobility during the dry season. This includes pastoralists who move their cattle during the dry season to wetter areas in the south (Ballo 2009; Hein et al. 2009) and labour migrants who move from rural areas to economically important rural and urban areas when there is less agricultural work at home. Notably male migration has a long tradition and is often attributed to the environmental conditions in the region, while the independent migration of unmarried women is a more recent phenomenon (Adepoju 2005; Bakewell and de Haas 2007; Sieveking and Fauser 2009). Migration from the rural areas in the Sahel is often explained through narratives in which rural inhabitants migrate in response to negative (push) factors such as environmental change, population growth, increasing economic pressure or the lack of opportunities at home. However, positive (pull) factors, such as the demand for labour forces in economic centres, have also influenced migration behaviour (de Haan et al. 2002).

Interviewing the people from Bandiagara in Mali and Linguère in Senegal

Bandiagara in Mali and Linguère in Senegal (see Figure 2.1) are two rural areas in the West African Sahel. The two areas have been chosen for empirical research on the linkages between environmental change and migration for the following reasons. Both areas show noticeable signs of environmental change including highly variable precipitation, change in vegetation cover, land degradation and the strong likelihood of experiencing droughts in the future. They are relatively poor rural areas where the majority of the people depend on small-scale agricultural activity as main source of income. As a result, the effects of environmental stressors are presumed to be particularly high and visible in these areas. Moreover, both rural areas show a high rate of population mobility with a negative net migration balance, meaning that the number of people who depart from the regions is higher than those arriving. The comparison of two different rural study areas in Mali and Senegal with similar climatic conditions and migration patterns helps to identify local specifications and generalizable results for the West African Sahel.

The two study areas also differ in some aspects, for instance, in landscape and farming conditions. In the Linguère region, the landscape consists of dry grassland with scattered trees and bushes as well as low vegetation diversity

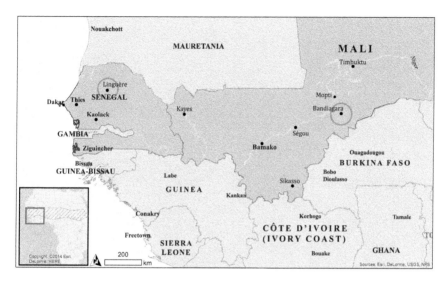

Figure 2.1 The study regions: Linguère in Senegal and Bandiagara in Mali.

(Hein et al. 2009). The Malian study area is geographically divided into the "Dogon Plateau" around Bandiagara, and the "Séno Plain" around Bankass, which stretches southwards from Bandiagara. The soils on the plateau are sandy and lateritic with rocky sandstones in certain places, while the Seno plain sands are deep and infertile (Brandt and Romankiewicz et al. 2014). The droughts of the 1970s and the 1980s caused considerable damage in the region resulting not only in severe food shortages, but also in a remarkable reduction of vegetation diversity and tree density.

The Linguère region in Senegal is a silvo-pastoral zone, inhabited by semi-nomadic Fulani pastoralists, but also by farmers who mainly belong to the ethnicity of the Wolof. The main ethnic group around Bandiagara in Mali are the Dogon, traditional farmers. Millet, groundnut and sorghum are the main arable crops in both areas. Approximately 90% of inhabitants in both countries follow Islam with polygamous marriage still common in rural areas. The inhabitants of Bandiagara and Linguère are among the poorest in their countries: only a minority of the population has access to basic social services, such as education, health services, fresh water and electricity. During the past 50 years, drought and soil erosion as well as population growth, human expansion and increasing resource use have led to an increase of cultivated areas, overexploitation and land degradation, particularly in the Malian region (MEA 2009) (Figure 2.2).

Empirical research of the two study areas includes quantitative and qualitative data collected in both rural areas, as well as in the capitals of Bamako and Dakar. A combination of qualitative and quantitative data, thus a mixed methods approach, was chosen in order to gain a better understanding of the

Figure 2.2 A Dogon village in Mali.
Source: Author.

livelihood conditions and migration patterns in both areas by combining different perspectives. Research on-site took place over the course of five months, including an explorative phase from February to April 2011 and a main field phase from January to April 2012 in Mali and in Senegal, thus, prior to the political crisis in Mali.

A standardised quantitative migration survey with 905 people was conducted in the research project, which included 445 in Mali and 460 in Senegal. Two-thirds of the questionnaires were completed with villagers in the two rural study areas of Bandiagara in Mali and Linguère in Senegal (total n = 661) and approximately one-third with migrants from these areas in the two capitals, Bamako and Dakar (total n = 244). The survey includes individuals aged 18 years or older who originate from the districts of Linguère in Senegal and Bandiagara in Mali, with and without personal experience of migration – but excludes nomadic transhumance. The sampling of the survey participants is based on a quota sample with an equal distribution of men and women in three different age groups. In the two capitals, migrants from the two rural areas were identified using a snowball sampling method. A random sample was difficult to realise due to a lack of a population frame, but a comparison of the results with national census data suggests that the survey data can be considered as nearly representative. The survey data aims to describe the economic situation and migration patterns of the study areas through quantitative analysis and to detect relationships between migration behaviours and individual characteristics by applying chi-squared (χ^2) tests and a significance level of 0.05.

In addition to the survey, the findings derive from 59 qualitative semi-structured interviews conducted in Bandiagara and Linguère, as well as with migrants from these areas in the capitals, Bamako and Dakar. This includes 26 interviews with Malians and 33 interviews with Senegalese. Most interviews were conducted in local languages and translated into French. For this book, the citations are translated from French into English by the author. The qualitative interviews analyse people's personal experiences, perceptions and aspirations in relation to migration. The book refers to the quantitative data by using the term "survey" and to the qualitative data by using the term "interview." It further uses the terms "Malians" and "Senegalese" synonymously for the people from the respective study areas in the interest of readability. Both the survey and interviews focused on the individual and her/his migration motives, needs and aspirations, in addition to the common household perspective. This focus aims to add a new perspective to the environment-migration research, in which the household usually represents the main unit of analysis.

Livelihood conditions, environmental stressors and people's adaptation strategies

Agriculture is the main economic activity for people from the rural areas of Linguère and Bandiagara. Specifically, arable farming and livestock breeding are the main economic activities for 67% of the survey participants interviewed in the rural study areas and for 93% of their families. The main form of agriculture in both rural areas is arable farming with millet, groundnut and sorghum as the main crops. In the Linguère region in Senegal, the most common agricultural activities are crop production (43% of survey participants) and livestock breeding (23% of survey participants) (see Figure 2.3). The share of livestock breeders is relatively high in Senegal compared to the Malian study area because it is a silvo-pastoral zone inhabited by many semi-nomadic Fulani pastoralists who live side by side with farmers that primarily belong to the Wolof ethnicity. The Bandiagara region in Mali, in contrast, is mainly inhabited by farmers who belong to the Dogon ethnicity and, to a much lesser extent, by livestock-herding Fulani pastoralists. Thus, it is not surprising that arable farming is by far the main economic activity for 73% of survey participants in the Malian study area. Other main economic activities in the Malian region are domestic work, handicraft and irrigated vegetable gardening. Trading in commodities (18%) is an important economic activity in the Senegalese rural area. Almost all farmers in Bandiagara and Linguère indicate having a second source of income.

Migrants in the capitals depend almost exclusively on non-agricultural activities. Main activities for 66% of the migrants in Dakar are trading in commodities, such as car tires or agricultural products. Migrants in Bamako work as unskilled labourers (37%), in small business (26%) or in domestic work (19%).

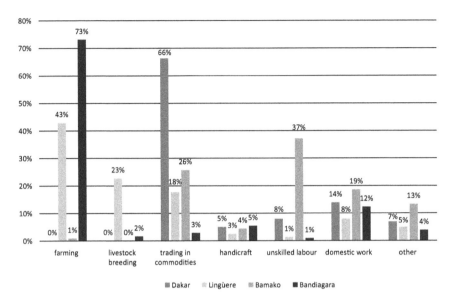

Figure 2.3 Main economic activities by region.

Source: Author.
Senegal n = 418, Mali n = 429; excluding students and inactive respondents.

Agriculture in the region heavily depends on the rainy season. The average annual precipitation is approximately 400 mm in the area around Linguère and 500 mm around Bandiagara, measured from 1950 to 2010 (Brandt and Romankiewicz et al. 2014). The rainy season normally occurs between July and September, but inter- and intra-annual rainfall is extremely variable in both areas. In Senegal, the average annual rainfall is 60 mm higher in the southern part of the relatively small research area of 50 x 50 km. Consequently, farmers mainly live in the southern part, while livestock breeders concentrate in the north.

Rainfall strongly varies between years and between study areas. In 2010, for example, rainfall was about 60% above the annual average in both study areas (GPCC/TRMM 1940 to 2012). In contrast, in 2011, rainfall was almost 20% below the annual average in the Linguère area, while it was slightly above average in the area around Bandiagara (Brandt and Verger et al. 2014). In general, rainfall has slightly increased during the last years compared to previous decades. Nevertheless, people predominantly perceived negative changes in the quantity and variability of rainfall over the last 20 to 30 years – compared to the years before the droughts. Malian respondents generally perceived the changes in rainfall more negatively than respondents from the Senegalese study area, who often assessed the changes as naturally variable. Some 71% of the Malian survey participants indicated a decrease in rainfall compared to 55% of the Senegalese. Similarly, the same percentage of Malians perceived an increase of interruptions in rainfall compared to 36% of the Senegalese.

The amount and quality of rainfall strongly influences people's harvests and yields, thus, their food security. While food security is a major risk in the area, it does not only depend on rainfall conditions. In 2011, a year with poor rainfalls, 75% of Senegalese farmers and 69% of Malians indicated that the yields were insufficient to nourish their family. Surprisingly, the Malians and the Senegalese almost equally assessed the outcome from crop production and livestock breeding, even though rainfall was below average in Senegal and average in Mali. Even in years with excellent conditions for precipitation, the agricultural production was not sufficient to ensure food security. Despite the strong rainy conditions in 2010, some 60% above average in both areas, farmers indicated that the yields were insufficient to nourish their family (28% from Senegal versus 53% from Mali, respectively). A possible explanation is that floods caused by heavy rainfalls in Mali in 2010 might have had negative effects on yields and pasture. Another possibility is that the Senegalese might have developed more effective strategies to cope with food shortages.

Although rain plays a crucial role for the success of the yields, other impact factors also influence the yields negatively. A variety of factors negatively influenced the yield in 2011 (see Figure 2.4). During that year, the lack and uneven distribution of rainfall were the main impact factors on people's yields. Nevertheless, other limiting factors mentioned by the survey participants were the lack of fertiliser, the lack of agricultural equipment and unsatisfying soil fertility. In Senegal, crop pests and the lack of seeds were relevant impact factors for the yields, while they barely played a role in Mali.

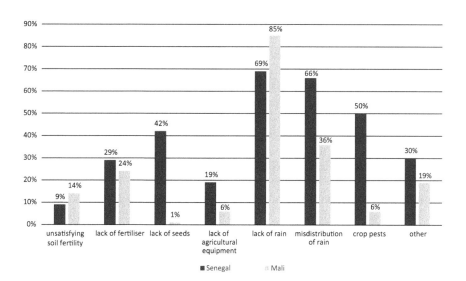

Figure 2.4 Negative influencing factors for the yields in 2011.

Source: Author.
Senegal n = 384, Mali n = 436, only respondents with farming activities; multiple answers possible.

According to most interviewees, the conditions for agriculture have worsened during the last 20 to 30 years. A combination of factors negatively influences the agricultural outcome and differs between the two rural areas. In Senegal, people emphasised the devastating effects of crop pests, such as locust and bird invasions on the yields. In Mali, decreasing soil fertility caused by land overuse as a consequence of population growth and a lack of access to additional fertile land negatively influence the yields. At 3%, the population growth rate is high in both countries. The population density, however, differs strongly between the two areas. There are approximately 16 people per km² in the area around Linguère compared to 64/km² in Senegal (ANSD 2010). With 30 people per km² in the Malian study area, the pressure on the land is much higher in Mali (INSTAT 2011). To make things worse, parts of the rocky soil on the Malian Dogon plateau are not suitable for arable farming and the lack of financial means for fertiliser often worsens the situation. According to the survey results, 33% of Malians indicated that they did not have sufficient land to cultivate. In contrast, availability of additional land in the Senegalese study area was less problematic, only 8% indicated not having sufficient land.

Although the lack and high variability of rainfall are major stressors of people's livelihoods and food security, climate and environmental changes are not the only factors to worsen the conditions for agriculture. Stressors, such as the lack of fertiliser, lack of agricultural equipment, access to land or effective measures against crop pests are often a result of poverty. The variety of stressors causes a lack of food [French: "manque de nourriture", author] and a lack of financial means [French: "manque de moyens", author], which are the major problems in both rural areas indicated by the people.

Over time, people living in West African Sahel have developed strategies to deal with the harsh environmental conditions in order to cope with food security and a lack of financial means. Particularly, the diversification of income sources is an important means for individuals and households to reduce the risks from crop failure and (future) external stress (Davies 1996). In the rural areas around Bandiagara and Linguère, almost all farmers (90%) have a second source of income. Income diversification can be realised by local activities or by migration. A common local activity in both areas is combining crop production with livestock breeding. Investment in livestock after good harvests allows coping for future risks. To compensate for years with poor yields, selling part of their livestock is the most common strategy for 63% of the households and almost equally important in both countries (see Figure 2.5). Other strategies include selling natural products, like wild fruits, herbs and straw (15%) and wood or carbon (10%). In Mali, irrigated gardening is a common activity to complement the income from agriculture. Vast fields of shallots, onions and tomatoes, mainly financed by development aid organisations, cover the Dogon plateau. In addition, the solidarity among the villagers is an important strategy to compensate for poor yields in both countries: one-third indicated receiving help from other community members when yields are insufficient. Nevertheless, the Senegalese rely, to a higher percentage, on the solidarity of others than the Malians (43% versus 21%).

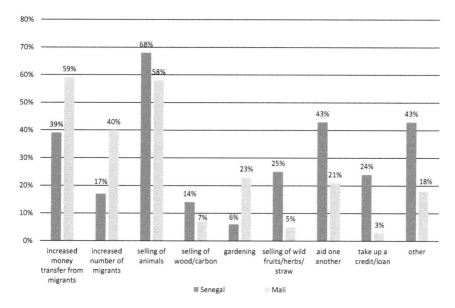

Figure 2.5 Strategies to compensate poor yields or pasture conditions.
Source: Author.
Senegal n = 411; Mali n = 443; multiple answers possible.

The strategies available on-site are limited. Both rural areas offer little alternative local employment opportunities outside of agriculture, which often leaves migration as the only available and, in many cases, the most effective option to spread the risk of food insecurity. Family members in migration increase the amount of money they send back home (49%) and/or more members of a household migrate (29%) when the harvest and pasture conditions are assumed to be poor. Migration-related strategies seem however to be more common in Mali, whereas the Senegalese rely on the aid of other family or community members, take up a credit or loan, or engage in other economic activities. Other strategies include different kinds of petty trade or economic activities, such as carriage driver or guardian. Most of the local livelihood activities in the rural areas depend on the natural environment and thus may not be very effective in the case of extreme environmental events. This makes migration a particularly important livelihood activity.

Households usually have a whole range of different income sources of which the financial support of household members in migration is only one, but a very important one, because it does not depend on the natural environment. The following citations from Modou, a young Senegalese farmer, illustrates the variety of income sources and livelihood strategies applied by the households in the study areas:

> We cannot any longer live from arable farming alone because it is insufficient. That is why we breed livestock as well. It allows us to have other

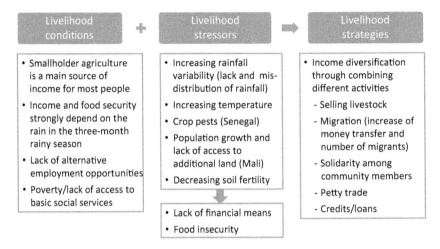

Figure 2.6 Livelihood conditions, stressors and strategies in the rural areas around Bandiagara and Linguère.

Source: Author.

sources of income to satisfy our food needs. I do have another job to cover our daily expenditures and we do some commodity trading in order to help our family. In addition, my brother sends us money.

(Modou/30 years/male/Senegal)

To sum up, people in both study areas rely heavily on smallholder agriculture as their main source of income. This makes them particularly vulnerable to environmental stressors. Food insecurity is the main risk for people's livelihoods and often considered a key cause of migration. But people have developed several strategies to cope with the harsh environment. Although migration might be an important activity, not all people may consider migration as a livelihood strategy. Figure 2.6 summarises the findings on people's livelihood conditions, stressors and activities in the two study areas.

Mobility as common activity in the West African Sahel: experiences and patterns

Migration is very common in both rural study areas in Mali and Senegal. The majority of the survey participants (81%) have personal migration experience. This means that they left their area of origin at least once for a minimum of three months. Most people, however, had left their area at least twice (70%). Migration is slightly more common among Malians than Senegalese (86% versus 79%). With respect to gender, migration experience does not differ between men and women from Senegal, while migration experience is more common among men than among women in Mali, with 94% versus 70%, respectively. The share of Malian women with migration experience still appears surprisingly high compared to the findings of earlier studies and national statistics on female migration from the Dogon country, and considering that female migration is a rather new phenomenon (Ballo 2009; Sieveking and Fauser 2009; INSTAT 2012). The commonality of migration supports the view that migration is the norm rather than the exception and suggests that environmental stress is not the only reason for migration from the two environmentally fragile areas.

Surprisingly, migration is common among almost all people from the two rural areas and does not differ by economic activity or by other socio-demographic characteristics, such as age or level of education. There is no indication on whether or how migration flows have changed over the last decades. The same percentage of young and elderly participants indicated personal migration experiences, yet migration from rural areas frequently takes place at a young age. Most rural villages are void of young people, leaving only elderly people and children, particularly during the dry season. When people first left the rural study area, they were on average 18 years old in Senegal and one year older in Mali, with no considerable differences between men and women. In both countries, women were younger than men when they last migrated, with an average of 27 years compared to an average of 33 years among men. This is because women primarily migrate before marriage.

Migration from both rural areas is mainly circular migration either within the country or to neighbouring countries. Migrants from both areas maintain strong ties with their home community and visit their village frequently or even return home at some point. Many male migrants also still have their family, including wife or wives, children and parents, in the village. The family remains in the village due to traditional reasons, such as a strong attachment to the land and the traditional role of the wife/wives to support the mother-in-law. Families also often remain in the village because living costs are lower in rural areas than in cities. Migrants living in the capitals often considered themselves as living in the village, even though they spent most of their time working and living in destination areas. Many of them expressed their wish to return to the village for retirement, even those who have been living with their family in the city for decades.

When people first left the area, they usually returned after a period of time. Most Senegalese returned after a short period of three to under 10 months (40%), while Malians mostly stayed for a longer time, from 10 months to under five years (46%). Less than one-third of the migrants left for five years or longer, with 33% in Senegal and 14% in Mali. Migration patterns differ considerably between men and women, particularly in the Malian study area (see Table 2.1). Women in Mali migrate significantly more often for a longer period of time than their male counterparts who mainly migrate for a short period. The duration of migration depends on many different factors, such as the reasons for migration, the type of labour engaged during migration, the financial gains and the number of people of working age in the household.

Today mobility in West Africa mainly takes place within a country or within the sub-region of West Africa. In Senegal and Mali, internal migration accounts

Table 2.1 Duration of people's first migration by country (shares in percent).

Duration	Country					
	Senegal			Mali		
	Men (n = 209)	Women (n = 168)	Total (n = 377)	Men (n = 268)	Women (n = 128)	Total (n = 396)
Short-term (3 to < 10 months)	43	36	40	49	22	40
Temporary (10 months to < 5 years)	25	31	28	41	54	46
Permanent (5 years and longer)	32	33	33	9	24	14

Source: Author.

for the largest percentage of movements, which are mainly directed from rural to urban areas (Guèye et al. 2007; ANSD 2009). Senegal, historically an immigration country for other Africans, turned into an emigration country in the early 1980s and into a transit country for migrations to the Maghreb and European countries (Some 2009; Di Bartolomeo et al. 2010). While Senegalese emigration in the past has primarily been migration to other African countries, the economic and political instability of neighbouring countries in the 1990s led to a change towards intercontinental migration, with Europe as the main destination (MEF 2004). In contrast to Senegal, Mali has traditionally been one of West Africa's typical emigration countries and is an important transit country for West Africans migrating to North Africa and/or to European countries.

Today, more than one-third of Senegalese emigrants and 20% of Malian emigrants move to countries in the "North", mostly to Europe with France, Italy and Spain as the main destinations (Di Bartolomeo et al. 2010; INSTAT 2012). The majority of the emigrants, however, migrate to other African countries. Remittances from emigration are an important source of income in both countries. In Senegal, they have tripled during the last 10 years; reaching US$ 1.6 billion in 2013. Remittances are mainly sent from the "North" (70%) and are higher than the country's Official Development Assistance (ODA) and the amount of Foreign Direct Investment (FDI) inflows (The World Bank 2010). The Malian emigrants remitted an estimated US$ 842 million in 2013, a number that has quintupled during the last 10 years. The amount has been mainly remitted (67%) from countries from the "South" and although it was not higher than the

Overseas Development Assistance (ODA), it has been higher than the Foreign Direct Investment (FDI) (The World Bank 2010, 2014)

From the two rural study areas in Senegal and Mali, most people chose a destination within the country. In Senegal, almost all migrants moved within the country. In contrast, from the Malian area, one-third moved to neighbouring countries, mostly to Cote d'Ivoire. Of those people who stayed within the country, about one-third went to the capital of their home country and only a few people stayed in the districts of Linguère and Bandiagara. In Senegal, long-distance destinations to the rural districts of Kaolak, Tambacounda and Matam were common (see Table 2.2). Women mainly migrated to the capital of their country. International and sub-regional migration was mainly restricted to men with only a few women migrating across national borders.

Although one would expect a longer duration for a farther destination, there is no clear relationship between the duration and destination of migration. On the contrary, one-third of the Malians who left the country only stayed for a short period. This is surprising considering the time and cost related to the journey: a bus journey from Bandiagara in Mali to Abidjan takes almost two days and costs about a month's salary. Migration patterns, both spatial and temporal patterns, might thus not only be influenced by the conditions in the area of origin but also by other factors.

The choice of the migration destination depends on many factors. Social networks play a crucial role for the choice of the destination because they facilitate the search for employment and accommodation. The majority of the surveyed migrants (82%) chose their first migration destination because they either had a friend or family member already present or knew somebody who

Table 2.2 Destinations of the first and last migration by gender and country (shares in percent).

Destinations	Country					
	Senegal			Mali		
	Men (n = 239)	Women (n = 172)	Total (n = 411)	Men (n = 337)	Women (n = 110)	Total (n = 447)
Within the country	93	96	95	59	87	66
- Capital	23	45	32	30	43	33
- Within the region of origin	13	16	14	17	36	22
- Long-distance destination	57	35	48	12	8	11
Outside the county	7	4	5	41	13	34

Source: Author.
Respondents in rural areas only; migration dataset.

had been there before. Social networks were more relevant for the choice of destination for Senegalese than for Malians (50% versus 32%, respectively). The interviews illustrate that international migration of Senegalese to Europe or the USA is restricted to the members of a few villages in the study area and strongly depends on their social networks. Women also rely heavily on social networks for their choice of destination (90% for women versus 73% for men). Girls are often sent to the household of other family members or friends to help them with their work, for education (not necessarily formal education) or to ease the pressure of the food available at home. Other factors that influence the migration decision are better professional and/or educational perspectives (40% for Senegalese versus 11% for Malians) or simply by chance (20% for Malians versus 3% for Senegalese). Additionally, 10% of respondents chose their migration destination because they wanted to get to know the city. The information on economic opportunities, such as access to jobs and expected profit in the destination area provided by previous migrants, also decisively influenced the choice of the destination as the following citation of Koala, a Malian migrant illustrates:

> I chose Abidjan because you can earn more money in Abidjan than in Bamako. (. . .) I heard this from the older people who left, those who leave and return. That is the reason why I wanted to go to Abidjan.
>
> (Koala/35 years/male/Mali)

Improvements of transport infrastructure, economic growth and employment opportunities influence the choice of destination in a positive way, while conflicts and political instability have a negative effect on the choice of destination (Bakewell and de Haas 2007). This is why migration destinations change over time and did so for people from both rural areas. Elder male interviewees from Mali explain that they used to migrate to Ghana in the early 1960s. Due to the economic and political crisis in 1966, people later directed their migration primarily to Cote d'Ivoire as a result of better employment opportunities. During the last decade, migration destinations outside the country decreased slightly from the Malian study area, probably due to the civil war and political crisis in Cote d'Ivoire (2002–07 and 2010–11).

In Senegal, migration to rural areas, such as Saloum, Kaolak, Fouta, Matam or Podor, has changed to urban areas, such as Dakar, Thiès and Mbour, and to international destinations, which had not been accessible at earlier times. According to the interviewees, migration from the Senegalese study area to Europe started in the 1980s, but decreased in recent years due to the financial crisis in Europe and the related difficulties of finding employment, as well as more restrictive migration policies of "Western" countries. Moreover, return migrants from international destinations interviewed in Senegal concordantly explained that they strongly discourage other household and community members to leave the continent due to their own "suffering" in migration. International migration might still be a dream for some young men in Senegal but stories of failed migration, awareness campaigns about the risks and costs of illegal migration, as well as a strong discouragement from those who had succeeded to arrive in Europe, made it less desirable. For the Malians, migration across continents seemed more uncommon due to higher costs and less available means.

Bibliography

Adepoju, A. 2005 *Migration in West Africa: Global Commission on International Migration (GCIM)*.

ANSD 2009 *Situation économique et sociale du Sénégal en 2008*, Dakar: Agence Nationale de la Statistique et de la Démographie (ANSD).

ANSD 2010 *Situation économique et sociale de la région de Louga 2010*, (Service Régional de la Statistique et de la Démographie: Louga), Agence Nationale de la Statistique et de la Démographie (ANSD).

Bakewell, O. and de Haas, H. 2007 "African migration: Continuities, discontinuities and recent transformation", in Chabal, P., Engel, U. and de Haan, L. eds. *African alternatives*, Leiden: Brill, 95–118.

Ballo, M. 2009 *Migration au Mali: Profil national 2009*, Geneva: International Organization for Migration (IOM).

Brandt, M., Romankiewicz, C., Spiekermann, R. and Samimi, C. 2014 "Environmental change in time series – an interdisciplinary study in the Sahel of Mali and Senegal" *Journal of Arid Environments*, 105, 52–63.

Brandt, M., Verger, A., Diouf, A., Baret, F. and Samimi, C. 2014 "Local vegetation trends in the Sahel of Mali and Senegal using long time series FAPAR satellite products and field measurement (1982–2010)" *Remote Sensing*, 6(3), 2408–2434.

Cordell, D.D., Gregory, J.W. and Piché, V. 1996 *Hoe and wage: A social history of a circular migration system in West Africa* (African Modernization and Development Series), Boulder, CO: Westview Press.

Davies, S. 1996 *Adaptable livelihoods: Coping with food insecurity in the Malian Sahel*, New York: St. Martin's Press; Macmillan Press.

de Haan, A., Brock, K. and Coulibaly, N. 2002 "Migration, livelihoods and institutions: Contrasting patterns of migration in Mali" *Journal of Development Studies*, 38(5), 37–58.

de Sherbinin, A., Levy, M., Adamo, S., MacManus, K., Yetman, G., Mara, V., Razafindrazay, L., Goodrich, B., Srebotnjak, T., Aichele, C. and Pistolesi, L. 2012 "Migration and risk: Net migration in marginal ecosystems and hazardous areas" *Environmental Research Letters*, 7(4), 1–14.

Di Bartolomeo, A., Fakhoury, T. and Perrin, D. 2010 *CARIM – migration profile Senegal*. Consortium for applied research on international migration.

Guèye, C., Fall, A.S. and Tall, S.M. 2007 "Climatic perturbation and urbanization in Senegal" *The Geographical Journal*, 173(1), 88–92.

Hammer, T. 2004 "Desertification and migration: A political ecology of environmental migration in West Africa", in Unruh, J.D., Krol, M.S. and Kliot, N. eds. *Environmental change and its implications for population migration*, Dordrecht, The Netherlands: Kluwer Academic Publishers, 231–246.

Hein, L., Metzger, M.J. and Leemans, R. 2009 "The local impacts of climate change in the Ferlo, Western Sahel" *Climatic Change*, 93(3–4), 465–483.

INSTAT 2011 *Série démographique, 4ème recensement général de la population et de l'habitat du Mali* (RGPH-2009), Institut National de la Statistique du Mali.

INSTAT 2012 *Accessibilité aux soins de santé, mobilité, vie politique et associative et dépenses de consommation des ménages: juillet-septembre 2011.* Rapport d'analyse deuxième passage (Enquête modulaire et permanente auprès des ménages (EMOP)), Bamako, Mali: Institut National de la Statistique du Mali.

IOM 2014 *IOM regional strategy West and Central Africa 2014–2016*, International Organization for Migration (IOM).

IPCC 2007 *Climate change 2007: The physical science basis. Contribution of working group I to the fourth assessment report of the intergovernmental panel on climate change*, Cambridge and New York: Cambridge University Press.

IPCC 2013 *Climate change 2013: The physical science basis: Contribution of working group I to the fifth assessment report of the intergovernmental panel on climate change*, Cambridge and New York: Cambridge University Press.

MEA 2009 *Evaluation integrée des Ecosystèmes: Cas de la Région de Mopti au Mali*, Bamako, Mali: Ministère de l'Environnement et de l'Assainissement.

MEF 2004 *Rapport de synthese de la deuxieme enquete senegalaise aupres des menages* (ESAM-II), Dakar, Senegal: Ministere de l'Economie et des Finances: Direction de la Prévision et de la Statistique.

Mertz, O., Mbow, C., Reenberg, A., Genesio, L., Lambin, E.F., D'haen, S., Zorom, M., Rasmussen, K., Diallo, D., Barbier, B., Moussa, I.B., Diouf, A., Nielsen, J.Ø. and Sandholt, I. 2011 "Adaptation strategies and climate vulnerability in the Sudano-Sahelian region of West Africa" *Atmospheric Science Letters*, 12(1), 104–108.

Mortimore, M. and Adams, W.M. 1999 *Working the Sahel: Environment and society in northern Nigeria* (Routledge research global environmental change series 2), London, New York: Routledge.

OECD 2009 *West African studies regional atlas on West Africa.*

Rain, D. 1999 *Eaters of the dry season: Circular labor migration in the West African Sahel*, Boulder, CO: Westview Press.

Sieveking, N. and Fauser, M. 2009 *Migrationsdynamiken und Entwicklung in Westafrika: Untersuchungen zur entwicklungspolitischen Bedeutung von Migration in und aus Ghana und Mali* (COMCAD Working Papers 68), Bielefeld: Center on Migration, Citizenship and Development; Bielefeld University.

Sissoko, K., Keulen, H., Verhagen, J., Tekken, V. and Battaglini, A. 2011 "Agriculture, livelihoods and climate change in the West African Sahel" *Regional Environmental Change*, 11(S1), 119–125.

Some, N.A. 2009 *Migration au Senegal: Profil national 2009*, Geneva: International Organization for Migration (IOM).

The World Bank 2010 *Migration and remittances Factbook 2011.* 2nd edn., Washington, DC.

The World Bank 2014 *Migrant remittance inflows – data.*

3 Theoretical perspectives on environment-migration research

The lack of a theoretical foundation

The environment-migration research is neither a scientific discipline in itself nor has it been attributed to a scientific discipline. Initially analysed by natural scientists and human geographers who wanted to attract attention to the risks of global warming, the topic became increasingly popular among social scientists and migration scholars, in particular. While earlier studies, promoted a unicausal relationship between environmental stress and population mobility, migration scholars argued that migration is multi-causal. As such, migration is usually not only influenced by environmental stress, but by the complex interplay of various factors such as cultural, demographic, economic, political or social aspects. Empirical studies have been classified to two conceptual categories accordingly (Jónsson 2010): a) studies which use a push-pull framework that assumes an unidirectional link between environmental changes and migration; and b) approaches that consider the multi-causality of migration. Although researchers today widely agree on the multi-causality of migration, the research designs applied in recent West African case studies still assume to a greater or lesser extent environmental push and pull factors of migration (van der Land et al. forthcoming). The unsatisfying persistence on push-pull frameworks might result from a lack of theory and concepts in the field, which in turn could be caused by the absence of affiliation to a particular discipline.

Empirical case studies on the environment-migration nexus hardly link their research to current theories and concepts, thus lack theoretical foundation. Studies that contain any kind of theoretical or conceptual framing of environment-migration research can be classified into two groups. The first group of researchers attempted to elaborate a specific conceptual framework for the environment-migration research (see e.g. McLeman and Smit 2006; Adamo 2008; Perch-Nielsen et al. 2008; Foresight 2011; Kniveton et al. 2011; Renaud et al. 2011; Schmidt-Verkerk 2011; Scheffran et al. 2012; Rademacher-Schulz et al. 2012; Warner et al. 2012). Despite a variety of attempts, none of the proposed conceptual frameworks has been successfully established in the research on the environment-migration nexus. Most frameworks focus on climate change or environmental hazards as starting points of migration, instead of understanding migration as multi-causal phenomenon that is embedded in a broader context. Moreover, they usually do not consider that people dispose a portfolio of several local strategies to respond to external stress and that "staying" could be an alternative to migration. The most convincing and most cited approach is probably the conceptual framework of the drivers of migration developed in the "Foresight" project (Foresight 2011; Black and Adger et al. 2011). The Foresight-framework considers the multi-causality of migration, the role of migrants as active agents and understands migration as one possible response to environmental stress among others. Nevertheless, it presumes that external stressors drive migration, limiting people's agency to a reactive response to cope or adapt to environmental stress. Therewith, the framework widely disregards individual migration motives and aspirations to migrate that may influence migration even from areas affected by environmental changes.

A second group of researchers aimed to embed the research on migration and environment in contemporary theory or existing conceptual frameworks. Some migration scholars suggested treating the study of environment-migration issues as a part of migration research, framed by migration theories. However, this has only been realised by a few scholars (e.g. Ezra and Kiros 2001; Doevenspeck 2005). There was a tendency for environment-migration research not to consider migration theory – intentionally or unintentionally (Hummel et al. 2012). Other studies applied contemporary social theory such as the "theory of planned behaviour" (Kniveton et al. 2011) and Foucault's concept of power (Carr 2005). Several migration scholars have also argued that the impact of environmental change on migration is not determined by environmental factors themselves but by a lack of development that generates vulnerability to environmental change. Given the crucial role of development in the relationship between migration and environmental change and the strong conceptual parallels with development frameworks, several scholars have called to consider development theory and frameworks, such as household or livelihood approaches. Nevertheless, development frameworks, such as the Sustainable Livelihood Approach (SLA) or the Capability Approach (CA) have only been occasionally applied or mentioned in studies on the topic (e.g. UNDP 2009; Schmidt-Verkerk 2011; Scheffran et al. 2012; Schade 2013). Moreover, the conceptual frameworks of other studies suggests that they may have been inspired by livelihood research, but do not explicitly mention it (e.g. Foresight 2011; Gray and Bilsborrow 2013).

Migration as a livelihood strategy: what research may learn from (the critique on) livelihood studies

Livelihood research inspired the conceptual frameworks developed in environment-migration research, and therefore both research approaches have strong conceptual parallels. Both acknowledge the multi-causality of migration, focus on the household as main unit of the analysis and consider migration as a household strategy. In contrast to the environment-migration research with its narrow focus on migration caused by environmental stressors, livelihood approaches focus on the livelihood situation of households in a broader sense. This makes it difficult and time-consuming to apply them in practice. Livelihood studies consider an environmental stressor as only one of several external stressors that determine people's vulnerability. Moreover, they consider migration as an important livelihood activity, among others, to diversify the household's income. Migration and non-farming income was one of the cross-cutting themes applied to livelihood research since the end of the 1990s (Ellis 1998, 2003; Scoones 2009).

Box 3.1   The Sustainable Livelihood Approach

The Sustainable Livelihood Approach (SLA) is a common approach in development research and practice with the objective to improve the understanding of poor people's livelihoods and to reduce poverty (Chambers and Conway 1992; Scoones 1998; DFID 1999). Livelihood approaches have been developed as a critical response to the structural macro perspectives on development in the 1980s to analyse people's livelihoods and to better understand poverty. As a counterweight to the structural approaches to development, which tended to portray people as mere victims of structural constraints, the sustainable livelihood studies are actor-oriented. They highlight the agency of poor people to improve their livelihoods under certain structural conditions and have a positive view on people and development (Ashley and Carney 1999; Krantz 2001; de Haan and Zoomers 2005). Activities and research related to this framework are mainly carried out at a micro-level in developing countries, particularly in rural areas (Morse and McNamara 2013).

The livelihood approach offers two explaining dimensions with respect to migration. On the one hand, migration aims at reducing the risk and vulnerability to external stress and seasonality. On the other hand, it aims at improving the household's livelihoods and thus contributes to reduce poverty and to increase well-being (Ellis 2003). These two dimensions are also relevant for environment-migration research in the West African Sahel.

Environment-migration research refers to the first dimension of migration as a strategy to reduce risk and vulnerability to external stress. People in rural areas of developing countries mainly depend on agricultural economic activities and are often highly vulnerable to climate change and environmental stress. Migration combines farm and non-farm activities in order to diversify the household income even if economic opportunities on-site are limited. Migration from the rural areas of one or several household members often constitutes the only effective means to be able to cope with actual or future stress (Bebbington 1999;

McDowell and de Haan 2000). In the rural West African Sahel, the seasonality and high variability of rainfall are major threats to crop production and to people's income. Migration, particularly during the off-season, constitutes a common response to rainfall seasonality and supports the household's livelihoods in the region. By sending remittances back home to purchase additional food or even by not eating from the common pot, migrants ensure the household's food security (de Haan 2000).

The second dimension of migration in livelihood approaches is the contribution of migrant's remittances to reduce poverty and to increase the household's economic well-being. Environment-migration research often neglects this second dimension. As an activity to increase assets and to reduce poverty, migration is a proactive strategy based on choice and opportunity rather than a consequence of external stress (Ellis 1998). Farming alone often cannot satisfy the increasing need for cash; therefore, migration often constitutes the only or the most effective opportunity to accumulate financial means and to increase economic well-being. Remittances from migration can strengthen people's livelihood by investing in agriculture (e.g. land, seeds, fertiliser, material and hired labour), housing, mobility devices and consumer goods or education to improve prospects for the next generation. This second dimension of migration goes far beyond a survival strategy and household's basic needs. It is part of an accumulation strategy to improve livelihood and to reduce or overcome poverty (Bebbington 1999). Migration in the West African Sahel is a well-established livelihood strategy, which corresponds to history and cultural activity. It implies a notion of mobility as the norm rather than the exception and goes beyond economic needs. Environment-migration research should therefore consider that migration is not only a coping strategy to environmental stress, but also increases people's income thus contributing to a better life.

The two dimensions of migration in livelihood approaches – understanding of migration as an adaptation strategy as well as an opportunity to improve income – can be applied to environment-migration research. Moreover, a critique of the livelihood approaches may also contribute to advance conceptual frameworks and research in the field. There are two main critical arguments and weaknesses with respect to the livelihood approaches, particularly in relation to the Sustainable Livelihood Approach, that also apply to environment-migration research. The first critique relates to the focus on households and the second relevant critique refers to the view of migration as a strategic household decision and its focus on economic needs as reasons for migration.

The first critique of the livelihood approaches relates to the focus on the household as the analytical category. The household as unit of analysis has been considered as a compromise between agency and structure approaches (Bakewell 2010; de Haas 2010; Morse and McNamara 2013). However, considering the household as a monolithic and altruistic unit largely ignores unequal power relations, intra-household dynamics, conflicts within and between households as well as individual decision-making (Chant 1992; Waddington 2003; de Haan

2012). The focus on households assumes that decisions are based on a consensus between its members and are made to the advantage of the whole group. Instead, inequalities and conflicts between generations and genders are common within many households (Chant 1992; Kabeer 2003; Ruppert 2008; de Haas and Fokkema 2010).

In the Sahel societies, men and parents are attributed with more power in the household, compared to women and children, and thus decide over their own migration and the mobility of other family members. Age and gender are important factors to explain migration decision-making and migration processes. Household members with less power due to their age and gender might either be put under pressure to migrate or be excluded from migration (de Haas and Fokkema 2010). The individual's and the household's motives to migrate and the expected goals often conflict, particularly for temporary migration. The focus on households tends to disguise unequal power relations within the household and rules out the agency of individual household members and, hence, their potential ability to revolt against the will of powerful household members and change social structures (de Haas 2010).

Research within the environment-migration nexus has predominantly considered migration as a household strategy to adapt to environmental change. This presumes that the decision to migrate is agreed among all household members in the best interest of the whole household. This presumption ignores individual interests and motives for migration that are not identical or may even be conflicting with the household needs and interests. Moreover, it neglects that certain household members could be put under pressure to migrate or be excluded from migration.

The second critique relates to the focus on economic goals that ignore other reasons or objectives of migration. The livelihood approaches assume that people's behaviours are based on strategic decisions to maximise the economic benefit for the household, ignoring the influence of culture, emotions and altruism as well as individual interests and other non-economic benefits (Arango 2000; Schmidt-Verkerk 2011). Critics argue that the focus on migration as a strategic economic decision ignores non-economic reasons for migration that encompass people's "perceptions and ideas, their hopes and fears, their norms and values" (Kaag et al. 2004: 5). Furthermore, the focus on household's economic needs underestimates the importance of people's individual motives and ignores factors that people do not need for a livelihood but perceive as important to ameliorate their enjoyment of life, such as enhancing their social standing in the community or meeting expectations and aspirations (Goss and Linquist 1995; Morse and McNamara 2013).

The focus in environment-migration research on economic needs caused by environmental stressors also leaves little room for non-economic reasons of migration, such as education, adventure or experience. Even worse, it often equates economic reasons with economic needs to migrate. This neglects migration encouraged by economic opportunities elsewhere and that migration is a means to increase economic development. It limits people's agency to a response to structural causes and needs and ignores that people are likely to migrate towards opportunities rather than away from problems (Klute and Hahn 2007). The symptom of casting migration in developing countries as a development failure – instead of acknowledging its contribution to development – has been described as "sedentary bias" (Bakewell 2008). Although research acknowledges the migrant's agency in considering migration as an adaptation strategy to unfavourable conditions at home, it still neglects that people's migration from areas affected by environmental changes could be motivated by factors other than poverty or food insecurity. In contrast, migration research increasingly recognises the importance of non-economic goals and argues that approaches that focus on the economic goals of migration are suitable only to a limited extent in terms of explaining migration which takes place due to more personal reasons (Arango 2000; de Haas 2010). This might be true even for migration from environmentally fragile areas. The consideration of the household economic needs is certainly an important component of environment-migration research but should not be limited to it.

The aforementioned critiques show that the current exclusive view of migration as an adaptation strategy to reduce households' risks and vulnerability to environmental stress limits, and may mislead, empirical research. Moreover, the critique suggests that despite strong conceptual parallels, the Sustainable Livelihood Approach by itself would not be advantageous as a framework to explain the linkages between environmental change and migration. A suitable conceptual framework for research on the environment-migration nexus should therefore take into account several aspects. On the one hand, it should consider intra-household inequalities and power relations across gender and age for the migration decision. On the other hand, it should take into account the variety of reasons for migration, which includes individual motives, in addition to household motives, and economic opportunities and non-economic reasons for migration in addition to economic needs.

Individual choice and aspirations: building on the Capability Approach

A theoretical development framework that takes into account the above-mentioned critiques on the livelihood approaches and the environment-migration research is Sen's Capability Approach (CA). Amartya Sen's work on entitlements and capabilities has heavily influenced the livelihood research and the Sustainable Livelihood Approach. They have several conceptual parallels such as placing people at the centre of their framework and focussing on their agency. In contrast to livelihood research, the Capability Approach focuses on individuals, which allows consideration of different power inequalities among people and within a household. Moreover, it recognises that individual preferences influence people's choices and goes beyond economic and material considerations.

Box 3.2   The Capability Approach

The Capability Approach has been developed by Nobel laureate Amartya Sen and is based on his interpretation of "development as freedom" which is understood as the individual's freedom as the ultimate end and principal means of human development (Sen 2000). Sen's understanding of development goes beyond economic growth and is regarded as "a process of expanding the real freedoms that people enjoy" (Sen 2000: 3). In this view, the Capability Approach initiated a major change in development theory by shifting the analytical focus of development from growth of the gross national product to the people's freedoms (Sen 2000; Alkire and Deneulin 2009). The Capability Approach focuses on individual freedoms and (the expansion of) people's "capabilities" to lead the kind of lives they value and have reason to value. It thus focuses on what people are effectively able to do and to be, on quality of life and removing obstacles in people's lives (Robeyns 2005). Poverty is one major obstacle to people's development, which is why Sen considers it as capability deprivation.

Although the Capability Approach does not explicitly refer to the natural environment and environmental stress, it recognises that social and environmental factors can restrain people's capabilities to do and to be what they value. Environmental stressors can aggravate existing vulnerabilities and poverty and thus can be considered a form of capability deprivation. In addition, Sen has elaborated on the causes of famines extensively (Sen 1981, 2000). He focused on the economic power and substantive freedoms of individuals and families to produce or purchase food, thus their entitlement to food. Environmental stress or natural disasters can threaten people's food security by influencing their "endowments" or assets (e.g. land or labour), their "production possibilities" (e.g. employment opportunities, wage rates) and their "exchange conditions" (e.g. relative prices to sell and buy goods) (Sen 2000: 162–163). According to the Capability Approach, people have different options and capability sets, thus different possibilities to act. Environmental stress, therefore, affects people or certain groups or parts of a population differently (Sen 2015, 2000). Poverty or other (e.g. environmental) stressors restrain these options, while development enlarges the capability sets and their choices. People's preferences and aspirations decide which of the available options are chosen based on their capability set.

Attempts to use capabilities or aspects of the Capability Approach with respect to human mobility come from the literature on migration and development. The Human Development Report on human mobility and development states that mobility depends on and reflects people's ability to choose their preferred place of residence (UNDP 2009). Mobility or migration is chosen as a functioning of the capability set and is considered an essential component of people's freedom to lead lives they value and have reason to value. It includes the freedom to move as well as the freedom to stay in one's preferred location (UNDP 2009; de Haas and Rodríguez 2010). With respect to vulnerability, the UNDP report notes "vulnerability reflects threats to choices and capabilities (. . .). People are vulnerable when they lack sufficient core capabilities, since this severely restricts their agency and prevents them from doing things they value or coping with threats" (UNDP 2014: 23). Vulnerability to environmental and other external stress thus restricts people's capabilities to do or be what they value, including the decision to stay or to migrate. Human development in contrast aims at reducing people's vulnerability and to enlarge people's capabilities and choices (UNDP 2014). From the Capability Approach, migration can be analysed from a multi-faceted perspective reflecting an outcome of both the lack and possession of capabilities, depending on the socio-cultural context (Briones 2009). If people have the ability to choose between moving and staying, the migration decision is an expression of capabilities. If they cannot choose to stay, migration is a consequence of a lack of capabilities. In other words, mobility can constitute a necessity or a choice (UNDP 2009). Although there is considerable difference between migration out of choice and out of necessity, the distinction is not easy in practice.

The focus in the environment-migration research on the structural conditions, and thus mainly on the push-factors of migration could explain whether people have the capability to choose to migrate or stay. However, they cannot explain why some people migrate, and others do not, under similar (structural) conditions. Here, individual preferences and aspirations come into play. Individual preferences and aspirations usually determine the choice from the capability set (Carling 2002; Robeyns 2005; de Haas 2010). Individual aspirations include dreams, wishes, expectations, perceptions, taste and preferences.

Migration increases development and, in turn, economic and human development usually widen people's capabilities and increase their aspirations to migrate (de Haas 2007). Understanding migration as an expression of capabilities to realise individual aspirations could widen the narrow focus of environment-migration research that typically views migration as a household adaptation strategy to environmental stress.

Capabilities and aspirations: why people stay or migrate

Considering people's capabilities in the migration decision helps distinguish between people who actively decide to migrate or stay versus those who need to migrate or stay. People who need to migrate are considered as "forced migrants" while those who do not have the ability to move have been labelled as "involuntarily immobile" (Carling 2002) or "trapped populations" (Foresight 2011). These people have to stay or migrate against their preferences and aspirations because they do not have the capability to choose their preferred option. If people do have the capability to choose freely between different options, the selection of a certain action from the capability set occurs according to people's needs, preferences and aspirations. People's assets and their socio-economic position – often depending on individual characteristics – strongly influence whether people have the capability to choose between migrating and staying. The focus on people's aspirations not only explains why some people migrate while others stay despite living under similar conditions and facing similar environmental risks; it also challenges the view of migration in developing countries as an inevitable consequence of unfavourable living conditions.

Differentiating people's migration behaviour by their capability to choose freely between migrating and staying and their aspirations and preferences results in different types of people with respect to the migration "decision":

1   People who do have the capability to choose freely between staying and migrating: they usually decide by their preferences and aspirations for one or the other activity, and are either "voluntary migrants" or "voluntary immobile".
2   People who do not really have a choice to decide for one or the other but whose (only) possible option matches their preferences: they may not perceive themselves as being deprived of entitlements.
3   People who do not have the capability to choose between migrating and staying and whose preferences and/or aspirations are opposing the only available option: this includes those who are "forced" to migrate and those who are "trapped".

Figure 3.1 illustrates the different types of people by their capability and preferences to migrate or to stay, with type 1 reflected in the upper branch and type 3 in the lower branch. The figure shows that it is important to distinguish between not wanting and not being able to migrate or to stay. In practice, this could be difficult to determine in the context of slow-onset environmental changes. Even if the decision to move may technically be "voluntary", poor people may have no feasible alternative to migration.

The degrees of voluntariness between type 1 and 3 are manifold and should be imagined as a continuum (Hugo 1996; Hummel et al. 2012). Somebody might prefer to stay in the rural areas but employment elsewhere might offer more options other than low-paid local employment. Although the person chooses to migrate, the degree of freedom may not be the same as it would be for somebody who aspires to leave the rural area. People's preferences for a location or an activity and their individual aspirations for the future with respect to an occupation, lifestyle or economic situation may not be congruent and could require compromises. Nevertheless, their migration will imply a certain level of choice and agency, thus a voluntary character.

Migration characterised by type 3, however, does not usually imply any kind of agency but more likely a high pressure to leave the area or to stay. Recently, scholars of environment-migration research have emphasised that the "trapped" people are the most vulnerable to environmental stress because they are not able to use migration as an adaptation strategy (Black and Bennett et al. 2011; Black and Adger et al. 2011; Foresight 2011). These people thus lack the capability to

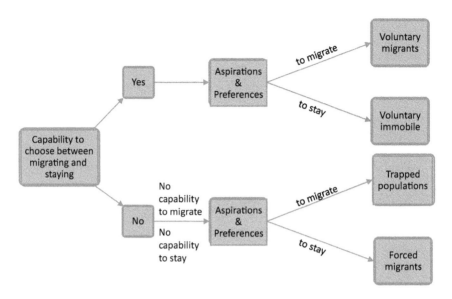

Figure 3.1 The influence of capabilities and aspirations/preferences on the migration decision and the level of voluntariness of migration.

Source: Author.

decide freely between migrating and staying. Black and Collyer specify that "to be 'trapped', individuals must not only lack the ability to move but also either want or need to move" (Black and Collyer 2014: 52). As a result, it is important to distinguish between not wanting and not being able to migrate. In the situation of environmental change, according to Black and Collyer, "low levels of capital indicate both high vulnerability to crises and low ability to move away" (Black and Collyer 2014: 54). Considering that poverty and vulnerability to environmental stress can be both an obstacle to migration and a root cause of migration (Skeldon 2002), low levels of capital indicate not only "a low ability to move away" but rather a low ability to choose freely between migrating and staying. Mobility or immobility can either be an expression or a lack of capabilities if restrained by environmental stressors or other factors.

The *Capability and Aspirations Approach*: a new conceptual framework

The new *Capability and Aspirations Approach* is a conceptual framework which aims to contribute to a better understanding of the linkages between slow-onset environmental changes and migration in the West African Sahel. Inspired by two development frameworks: the Sustainable Livelihood Approach (SLA) and the Capability Approach (CA), it also considers conceptual developments in the environment-migration research. The *Capability and Aspirations Approach* takes into account the social-ecological conditions for migration but focuses on the capability of people to migrate or to stay and their aspirations as core concepts. It illustrates that it is insufficient to focus on the structural (environmental) conditions alone to explain migration in areas affected by environmental changes. It not only challenges the view on migration in developing countries as an inevitable consequence of unfavourable living conditions, but also brings insights on why some people, faced with similar conditions and environmental risks, migrate while others stay.

The *Capability and Aspirations Approach* draws on the Sustainable Livelihood Approach (SLA) by considering both migration as a strategy to external stress, including environmental changes, and migration as an opportunity for economic gains. What differentiates the *Capability and Aspirations Approach* from the SLA, is that it focuses on individuals instead of households. Furthermore, not only does it consider economic goals, but also non-economic aspects as well as individual preferences and expectations as drivers of migration. The focus on individuals is helpful in drawing attention to people's capabilities, preferences and individual motives to migrate (or to stay). Inspired by Sen's Capability Approach, it can analyse how development entitles people to choose freely between migrating and staying and their ability to produce or purchase sufficient food, as well as provide insight on how far environmental stress may deprive people from these entitlements. Moreover, the new approach considers the outcome of migration on an individual and household level as well as social transformation processes that in turn also influence future migration decisions. Considering the individual perspective and multi-causality of migration avoids a simplistic conceptual push-pull that assumes a direct link between environmental stress and migration. Placing the individual at the centre of its analysis and attributing (more) agency to people by considering their aspirations and preferences challenges the "sedentary bias" in most existing approaches within migration and environment research in developing countries. The *Capability and Aspiration Approach* aims to overcome the differing notions of migration in the "North" and "South" as well as the restrained view on agency applied to the environment-migration nexus. Figure 3.2 illustrates the new conceptual approach, a generic tool to analyse the environment-migration nexus at the local level as well as on a national, regional and global level.

The *social-ecological context* represents the macro-level perspective of the new approach. The seasonality of rainfall, the lack of alternative local employment and other factors, such as a high population growth and a lack of additional accessible fertile land, migration culture, social norms and the level of development, shape the social-ecological conditions or context in the study areas. The social-ecological context determines people's capabilities as well as their preferences and aspirations to migrate and to stay and indirectly also the outcome of the migration decision. Environmental factors constitute only one aspect – among others – that shapes this context. In contrast to the "vulnerability context" in the SLA, which only refers to people's livelihood stressors,

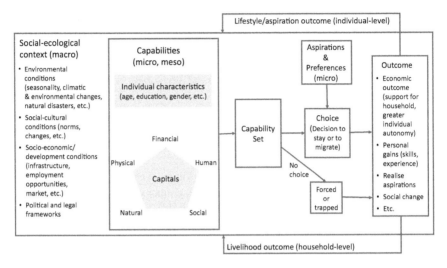

Figure 3.2 The *Capability and Aspirations Approach.*

Source: Author.

the social-ecological context includes also conditions that might positively influence people's livelihoods and reduce their vulnerability to environmental changes. It acknowledges that it is not satisfactory to focus on local (environmental) changes in the sending area, but that these changes and their impact on people's capitals have to be considered in a broader social context, including the relative opportunities elsewhere.

A person's *capabilities* to choose between migrating and staying or other livelihood activities depend on different factors: her/his individual characteristics, her/his own and the household's capitals at the meso-level. *Individual characteristics* such as age, gender, marital status, ethnicity or the level of education, do have different power implications with respect to the migration decision. In contrast to the current frameworks on the environment-migration nexus which suggest that individual characteristics influence the migration decision directly, the new conceptual approach highlights that individual characteristics influence the capabilities to choose between migrating and staying and the aspirations prior to the actual decision.

The *Capability and Aspirations Approach* takes into account the five forms of *capital* suggested by the SLA that refer to the individual's and the household's capitals. The *financial capital* can enable or inhibit migration. Climate and environmental change are likely to affect *natural capital*. Due to people's strong dependence on the natural environment, this also influences financial capital. *Physical capital*, including productive assets, such as land, tools and cattle can determine if additional income from other sources is needed. Migrant's remittances contribute to accumulated physical capital such as houses and community infrastructure, animals or tools. Extreme climate events can affect or destroy physical capital. *Human capital* includes skills, education, and health status, as well as the composition of the household. Education, knowledge, and skills increase people's options to work outside the agricultural sector and therefore reduce their vulnerability to environmental and other external risks (Francis and Hoddinott 1993; Ellis 2003; van der Land and Hummel 2013). Human capital also includes the composition of the household – number of male and female members and the number of people in working age – and their respective labour power. *Social capital*, especially in the form of social networks, facilitates migration and reduces the costs and risks of labour migration by providing access to accommodation and employment at the destinations (Massey et al. 1993; de Haas 2010).

In the social-ecological context, people's individual characteristics and their capital define their *capability set* that then determines if migrating and staying are available options. The *individual preferences and aspirations* are shaped by the social-ecological context and often depend on the individual characteristics. The preferences and aspirations usually determine the final migration decision if both options – leaving and staying – are available, even if they might be inspired by altruism. The *outcome* of this decision usually affects the household level and the individual level economically, but also in terms of gained knowledge and experience. The outcome, as a result, influences the social-ecological context and people's capability in a negative or positive way. This could lead to social changes that in turn influence people's migration decision.

The *Capability and Aspirations Approach* shapes the research for this book. The following chapters analyse people's motives to migrate and to stay. This includes food security as an indicator for environmental stress and household needs but also migration motives that suggest a more voluntary character of migration. The research gives special consideration to people's capabilities to decide to migrate or to stay, and their preferences and aspirations for one or the other. This is important to better understand who is particularly vulnerable to environmental stress and why some people migrate, while others stay, in the rural areas under harsh environmental conditions.

Bibliography

Adamo, S.B. 2008 *Addressing environmentally induced population displacement: A delicate task* (Background Paper for the Population-Environment Research Network Cyberseminar on "Environmentally Induced Population Displacements", 18–29 August 2008).

Alkire, S. and Deneulin, S. 2009 "The human development and capability approach", in Deneulin, S. and Shahani, L. eds. *An introduction to the human development and capability approach: Freedom and agency*, London: ebrary, Inc, 22–48.

Arango, J. 2000 "Explaining migration: A critical view" *International Social Science Journal*, 52(165), 283–296.

Ashley, C. and Carney, D. 1999 *Sustainable livelihoods: Lessons from early experience (Issues)*, London: UK Department for International Development.

Bakewell, O. 2008 "'Keeping them in their place': The ambivalent relationship between development and migration in Africa" *Third World Quarterly*, 29(7), 1341–1358.

Bakewell, O. 2010 "Some reflections on structure and agency in migration theory" *Journal of Ethnic and Migration Studies*, 36(10), 1689–1708.

Bebbington, A. 1999 "Capitals and capabilities: A framework for analyzing peasant viability, rural livelihoods and poverty" *World Development*, 27(12), 2021–2044.

Black, R., Adger, W.N., Arnell, N.W., Dercon, S., Geddes, A. and Thomas, D. 2011 "The effect of environmental change on human migration" *Global Environmental Change*, 21, S3–S11.

Black, R., Bennett, S.R.G., Thomas, S.M. and Beddington, J.R. 2011 "Migration as adaptation" *Nature*, 478, 447–449.

Black, R. and Collyer, M. 2014 "Populations 'trapped' at times of crisis" *Forced Migration Review*, 45, 52–56.

Briones, L. 2009 "Reconsidering the migration-development link: Capability and livelihood in Filipina experiences of domestic work in Paris" *Population, Space and Place*, 15(2), 133–145.

Carling, J. 2002 "Migration in the age of involuntary immobility: Theoretical reflections and Cape Verdean experiences" *Journal of Ethnic and Migration Studies*, 28(1), 5–42.

Carr, E.R. 2005 "Placing the environment in migration: Environment, economy, and power in Ghana's central region" *Environment and Planning*, 37, 925–946.

Chambers, R. and Conway, G.R. 1992 *Sustainable rural livelihoods: Practical concepts for the 21st century* (IDS Discussion Paper 296), Brighton: Institute of Development Studies.

Chant, S.H. ed. 1992 *Gender and migration in developing countries*, London, New York: Belhaven Press.

de Haan, A. 2000 *Migrants, livelihoods and rights: The relevance of migration in development policies*, Social Development Working Paper.

de Haan, L. 2012 "The livelihood approach: A critical exploration" *Erdkunde*, 66(4), 345–357.

de Haan, L. and Zoomers, A. 2005 "Exploring the frontier of livelihoods research" *Development and Change*, 36(1), 27–47.

de Haas, H. 2007 "Turning the tide? Why development will not stop migration" *Development and Change*, 38(5), 819–841.

de Haas, H. 2010 "Migration and development: A theoretical perspective" *International Migration Review*, 44(1), 227–264.

de Haas, H. and Fokkema, T. 2010 "Intra-household conflicts in migration decisionmaking: Return and pendulum migration in Morocco" *Population and Development Review*, 36(3), 541–561.

de Haas, H. and Rodríguez, F. 2010 "Mobility and human development: introduction" *Journal of Human Development and Capabilities*, 11(2), 177–184.

DFID 1999 *Sustainable Livelihoods Guidance Sheets 1*, UK Department for International Development.

Doevenspeck, M. 2005 *Migration im ländlichen Benin: Sozialgeographische Untersuchungen an einer afrikanischen Frontier*, Saarbrücken: Verlag für Entwicklungspolitik.

Ellis, F. 1998 "Household strategies and rural livelihood diversification" *The Journal of Development Studies*, 35(1), 1–38.

Ellis, F. 2003 *A livelihood approach to migration and poverty reduction*, UK Department for International Development.

Ezra, M. and Kiros, G.-E. 2001 "Rural out-migration in the drought prone areas of Ethiopia: A multilevel analysis" *International Migration Review*, 35(3), 749–771.

Foresight 2011 *Migration and global environmental change; Future challenges and opportunities* (Final Project Report), London: The Government Office for Science.

Francis, E. and Hoddinott, J. 1993 "Migration and differentiation in Western Kenya: A tale of two sub-locations" *The Journal of Development Studies*, 30(1), 115–145.

Goss, J. and Linquist, B. 1995 "Conceptualizing international labor migration: A structuration perspective" *International Migration Review*, 29(2), 317–351.

Gray, C. and Bilsborrow, R. 2013 "Environmental influences on human migration in rural Ecuador" *Demography*, 50(4), 1217–1241.

Hugo, G. 1996 "Environmental concerns and international migration" *International Migration Review*, 30(1), 105–131.

Hummel, D., Doevenspeck, M. and Samimi, C. 2012 *Climate change, environment and migration in the Sahel: Selected issues with a focus on Mali and Senegal* (micle – Working Paper 1), Frankfurt am Main: Institute for Social-Ecological Research (ISOE).

Jónsson, G. 2010 *The environmental factor in migration dynamics – a review of African case studies* (Working papers 21), Oxford: International Migration Institute (IMI). James Martin 21st Century School, University of Oxford.

Kaag, M., van Berkel, R., Brohns, J., Bruijn, M. de, van Dijk, H., de Haan, L., Nooteboom, G. and Zoomers, A. 2004 "Poverty is bad: Ways forward in livelihood research", in Kalb, D., Pansters, W. and Siebers, H. eds. *Globalization and development: Themes and concepts in current research*, Dordrecht, The Netherlands: Kluwer Academic Publishers, 49–76.

Kabeer, N. 2003 *Reversed realities: gender hierarchies in development thought*, London: Verso.

Klute, G. and Hahn, H.P. 2007 "Cultures of migration: Introduction", in Hahn, H.P. and Klute, G. eds. *Cultures of migration: African perspectives*, Münster: Lit, 9–27.

Kniveton, D., Smith, C. and Wood, S. 2011 "Agent-based model simulations of future changes in migration flows for Burkina Faso" *Global Environmental Change*, 21, S34–S40.

Krantz, L. 2001 *The sustainable livelihood approach to poverty reduction: An introduction*, Stockholm, Sweden: Swedish International Development Cooperation Agency.

Massey, D.S., Arango, J., Hugo, G., Kouaouci, A., Pellegrino, A. and Taylor, J.E. 1993 "Theories of international migration: A review and appraisal" *Population and Development Review*, 19(3), 431–466.

McDowell, C. and de Haan, A. 2000 *Migration and sustainable livelihoods: A critical review of the literature* (IDS Working Paper 65), Institute of Development Studies.

McLeman, R. and Smit, B. 2006 "Migration as an adaptation to climate change" *Climatic Change*, 76(1–2), 31–53.

Morse, S. and McNamara, N. 2013 *Sustainable livelihood approach: A critique of theory and practice*, Dordrecht, The Netherlands: Springer.

Perch-Nielsen, S., Bättig, M. and Imboden, D. 2008 "Exploring the link between climate change and migration" *Climatic Change*, 91(3–4), 375–393.

Rademacher-Schulz, C., Afifi, T., Rosenfeld, T., Milan, A., Etzold, B. and Sakdapolrak, P. 2012 *Rainfall variability, food security and human mobility: An approach for generating empirical evidence* (InterSecTions – Interdisciplinary Security Connections 10), Bonn: United Nations University Institute for Environment and Human Security.

Renaud, F.G., Dun, O., Warner, K. and Bogardi, J. 2011 "A decision framework for environmentally induced migration" *International Migration*, 49, e5–e29.

Robeyns, I. 2005 "The capability approach: A theoretical survey" *Journal of Human Development*, 6(1), 93–117.

Ruppert, U. 2008 " 'Gender makes the World go round': Frauenarbeit als Fundament von Weltentwicklung" *Forschung Frankfurt*, (3).

Schade, J. 2013 "Entitlements, capabilities and human rights", in Faist, T. ed. *Disentangling migration and climate change: methodologies, political discourses and human rights*, Dordrecht, The Netherlands: Springer, 231–253.

Scheffran, J., Marmer, E. and Sow, P. 2012 "Migration as a contribution to resilience and innovation in climate adaptation: Social networks and co-development in Northwest Africa" *Applied Geography*, 33, 119–127.

Schmidt-Verkerk, K. 2011 *The potential influence of climate change on migratory behaviour – a study of drought, hurricanes and migration in Mexico*. Dissertation. University of Sussex.

Scoones, I. 1998 *Sustainable rural livelihoods: A framework for analysis* (IDS Working Paper 72), Institute of Development Studies.

Scoones, I. 2009 "Livelihoods perspectives and rural development" *Journal of Peasant Studies*, 36(1), 171–196.

Sen, A. 1981 *Poverty and famines: An essay on entitlement and deprivation*, Oxford: Oxford University Press.

Sen, A. 2000 *Development as freedom*, New Delhi: Oxford University Press.

Sen, A. 2015 *Food, economics and entitlements* (WIDER Working Papers 1), World Institute for Development Economics Research, United Nations University.

Skeldon, R. 2002 "Migration and poverty" *Asia Pacific Population Journal*, 17(4), 67–82.

UNDP 2009 *Human development report 2009. Overcoming barriers: Human mobility and development*, New York: United Nation Development Programme.

UNDP 2014 *Human development report 2014. Sustaining human progress: reducing vulnerabilities and building resilience*, New York: United Nations Development Programme.

van der Land, V. and Hummel, D. 2013 "Vulnerability and the role of education in environmentally induced migration in Mali and Senegal" *Ecology and Society*, 18(4), 14.

van der Land, V., Romankiewicz, C. and van der Geest, K. forthcoming "Environment and migration – a review of West African case studies", in McLeman, R. and Gemenne, F. eds. *The Routledge handbook of environmental displacement and migration*, New York: Routledge.

Waddington, C. 2003 *Livelihood outcomes of migration for poor people*, Working Paper. Development Research Centre on Migration, Globalisation and Poverty, University of Sussex.

Warner, K., Afifi, T., Henry, K., Rawe, T., Smith, C. and Sherbinin, A. de 2012 *Where the rain falls: Climate change, food and livelihood security, and migration: An 8-country study to understand rainfall, food security and human mobility*. Global Policy Report, Bonn: CARE, United Nation University Institute for Environment and Human Security.

4 The role of environmental factors in shaping migration

Economic reasons as the main drivers of migration

Knowing that migration from both study areas is a common phenomenon raises the question about the reasons for migration. There is a consensus among environment-migration scholars that migration in areas affected by slow-onset environmental changes is multi-causal. The decision to migrate is usually influenced not only by environmental drivers but also by cultural, economic, political and social aspects (Laczko and Aghazarm 2009; Piguet et al. 2011; Hummel et al. 2012; Faist 2013; McLeman 2014). The terms *environmentally induced migration* or *environmental migrant*, however, imply that environmental factors are the main determinants for people's migration.

The *main* motive to leave the rural areas of both countries is economic reasons for 65% of the surveyed migrants. The survey inquired only about people's first migration, generally constituting the most profound decision, and last migration prior to the survey. Motives for the first and last migration did not differ significantly, thus they have been combined. The economic motive for migration is significantly higher than other motives, with 58% of migration linked to this motive in Senegal and 71% in Mali (see Figure 4.1). In the qualitative interviews people refer to economic reasons by using the terms "search for money/job opportunities" (in French: "chercher de l'argent/du travail" or "aller chercher") or "lack of means" (in French: "manque de moyens").

Surprisingly, environmental reasons were the main migration motive for only 15% of the migrants, with a higher percentage among the Senegalese than Malians (23% versus 6%). Environmental reasons for migration have been summarised by the category "food security" which comprises different issues including insufficient rainfall, unsatisfying soil fertility, lacking access to land and food insufficiency. Most people indicate that the yields had been insufficient to nourish the family and, to a lower extent, a lack of rainfall. Moreover, only 6% of the Senegalese indicate a lack of pasture as main migration motive, an indicator of environmentally induced migration for livestock breeders. This played no role at all in Mali. Other migration motives that received a limited response include: migration for tradition, health, tax, conflict, lack of access to water and religious reasons.

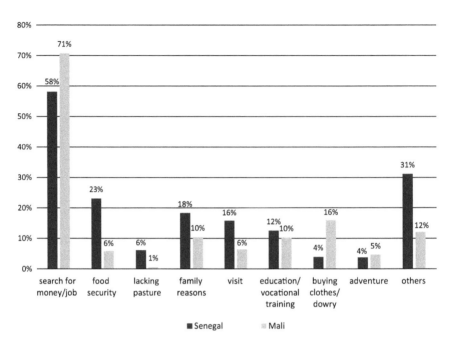

Figure 4.1 Main migration motives of people's first and last migration by country.

Source: Author.

Senegal n = 641; Mali n = 684; multiple answer possible; migration dataset.

The literature suggests that there are considerable differences in migration motives between men and women: Men usually migrate primarily for economic reasons while women migrate for marriage or other family reasons instead (Findley 1994; Ezra and Kiros 2001; de Haan et al. 2002; Henry et al. 2004; Dugbazah 2012; Hertrich and Lesclingand 2013). The differences in migration motives are rooted in traditional gender roles with the men's role to generate income and ensure the food security of the household (Chant 1992). Migration as a response to environmental stress is thus primarily attributed to men and usually linked to the need to sustain the household's food security.

In both rural areas in Mali and Senegal, men and women migrate primarily for economic reasons. The frequency is higher among men's migration compared to the women's migration (73% versus 49%), but is equally important for men from Senegal and Mali as well as for women from both areas. Surprisingly, men migrated only slightly more often than women for "food security" as the main migration motive. Despite the differences in migration motives between men and women, the results differ much more between the study areas than between genders. "Food security" as a main motive for migration is almost equally important for men and women from Senegal (24% and 21%), while it is low for both men and women from Mali (8% and 2%). Nevertheless, some migration motives differ between men and women. Women migrate much more often for family reasons than men (34% versus 4%), for "buying clothes/dowry" (19% versus 5%) and for "visits" (19% versus 5%). Men, in contrast, migrate more often for education and/or vocational reasons than women (15% versus 4%). This is not surprising since the share of women with formal education is still considerably lower than for men in both countries.

Although both men and women primarily migrate for economic reasons, the purpose for their economic migrations differs as illustrated by the following citation:

> The men provide the food and everything a woman earns is for herself. The women return with clothes and jewellery, but all this is for themselves.
>
> (Alioune/44 years/male/Senegal)

Men usually relate economic migration to their responsibility to support the family, including their economic well-being and food security. This confirms the ongoing importance of their traditional role as breadwinners. Men send part of their income back home to support the household but also use the money to build and maintain houses, to buy agriculture equipment or livestock or to buy consumer goods, such as motorcycles, clothes or mobile phones. Therefore, the economic migration of men not only contributes to cope with environmental stress and food insecurity, but also aims at accumulating financial means and improving the economic situation of the household and the migrant himself. Thus, migration not only includes the two dimensions of migration as a livelihood strategy, illustrated earlier in this book, but also a third dimension: fulfilling the migrant's economic aspirations. Women, particularly from Mali, specify that their economic migration aims to prepare for marriage, fulfil their own needs, and afford kitchen equipment, as well as acquire fashionable clothing and jewellery. They usually work as domestic workers or petty traders in the cities. Women, however, did not indicate to use the money to support the household's livelihood. Nevertheless, some young women shared their income with their mothers back home.

Migration as a routine to improve livelihoods

In the Sahel, circular, particularly seasonal, migration has a strong tradition in the rural areas, encouraged by the seasonality of rainfall. It has been described as a common supplemental economic activity to agriculture and/or an economic routine migration (Davies 1996; Ellis 2003; de Haan and Zoomers 2005). Interviews with elderly people confirm that seasonal migration is a well-established pattern in both areas for generations. The combination of a lack of work in agriculture during the dry season and the lack of alternative local employment opportunities in the rural areas favour migration. While environmental conditions in the region may have driven people to migrate in the first place, the gains from migration helped to establish migration as a routine economic activity. The goal is to accumulate financial means in order to cope with future external stress and to improve the migrant's and the household's economic situation. Today, tempo-rary migration mainly takes place independently from the quality of yields and is thus a routine migration rather than a response to environmental stress and poor yields.

> Even if the yields are good, people leave the area only just to gain more money. Even, if there is food, the money migrants earn increases.
>
> (Aly/36 years/male/Mali)

Elhadj, an elderly farmer from Senegal, explains the yearly alternation between farming and labour migration that is very common in both rural areas (see also Box 5.2). Every year after the rainy season, when the harvest is over, Elhadj leaves his village and his family to work at the fish market in Dakar. The labour activ-ity in Dakar is a regular supplemental economic activity to farming. Although migration takes place independently from the quality of the yields, the quality may determine the duration of his stay in Dakar.

> A good harvest may influence my behaviour a little bit and the activities I do. It may also reduce the time I remain in migration, but it cannot justify that I leave my profession.
>
> (Elhadj/60 years/ male/Senegal)

Today the members of most families in the two study areas are divided in two groups: one part of the family stays in the village, while other family members migrate to find employment in other parts of the country or neighbouring coun-tries. The division of the household in two groups is a strategy to diversify the household's income, minimising the risk of poor yields and food shortages. The migration of one or several household members is common in almost every household. Normally most working age male family members migrate for a cer-tain period, while the elderly, younger children, and often women stay in the village. Some family members return from migration for the harvest, while others continue to migrate to support the family with cash. Whether migrants return for the harvest or not, depends on the type of employment and contract, the revenues and the number of working age household members.

> Every family is divided into two groups: one group that stays in the village to cultivate what could result in poor yields and one group that works in the cities in order to support the family. If the yields are poor, the others in the city are obliged to support the family by sending money to the village.
>
> (Abdou/60 years/male/Senegal)

The migration of entire families is, however, very rare in both rural areas. People usually are strongly attached to their land due to its value and family tradition. By remaining in the rural areas, at least they possess land, whereas if the whole family migrated permanently, they would need to start from scratch in the destination area. The migration of young household members allows other family members, particularly elders, women and children to stay in the village. Members who stay in the rural area usually continue farming and often rely on the financial support of the migrant household members. An increasing number of household members in migration often results in a decrease of crop production due to a shortage of labour, but is usually compensated by the financial support of the migrants.

The migrants not only support the household with money, but also with food and clothes. The majority (86%) of the surveyed migrants and migrant households in both countries indicate that their household is supported by financial resources from migration. In Senegal, 58% state that the migrants provide the household with food, while it is less applicable in the case of Mali (22%). In contrast, 54% in Mali as opposed to 40% in Senegal indicate that the migrants provide clothing for the household.

Although the financial support of migrants is crucial for most households in both rural areas, it is often not a main driver but an important outcome of migration. Instead, the improvement of livelihoods and the accumulation of wealth and assets are important drivers of migration. Considering migration to be primarily an adaptation strategy to environmental changes implies only that people migrate in order to adapt to environmental risks and changes. It tends to neglect that people's migration might be motivated by the aim to accumulate assets in order to improve livelihoods and economic well-being, or by other motives.

The role of environmental stressors in economic migration

Environmental and economic factors that influence the migration decision are assumed to be particularly interdependent. Environmental changes can trigger or aggravate economic needs by negatively affecting agricultural productivity and rural livelihoods (Black et al. 2011). Usually, both unfavourable conditions in the sending area and positive (pull) factors, like the demand for labour forces in economic centres and opportunities in the receiving areas, encourage people to migrate. Nevertheless, environment-migration research still mainly focuses on the "push-factors" of migration, paying attention only to environmental drivers while widely ignoring that people might migrate in search of better economic opportunities.

Economic reasons are the main migration motives in both study areas and they may or may not be related to environmental stressors. Economic reasons for migration may indicate an economic need that could have been triggered by environmental stressors. Economic migration could also be a response to a lack of development and employment in the sending areas or it could be encouraged by economic opportunities elsewhere and be an expression of individual motives and aspirations. Most likely, it is a combination of all three. In order to identify the role of environmental factors behind economic migration motives, the survey inquired about people's main and secondary migration motives.

People's secondary migration motives show that environmental reasons often are closely linked to economic migration motives – at least in the Senegalese study area (see Table 4.1). In Senegal, 71% of the people who migrated for economic reasons, state food security as a secondary migration motive. In contrast, in Mali, only 13% of the economic migration has also been influenced by environmental reasons. Surprisingly, environmental reasons influenced almost half of the Senegalese migration (45%) as a main or secondary migration motive, while this applies to only 10% of the Malian migration. In general, "food security" was a more relevant migration motive for men than for women from the same area. In Senegal, 56% male migrants indicate "food security" as a main or secondary migration motive, followed by 30% of women's migrations. In Mali, "food security" as a migration motive was only relevant for 13% of men's migration, with 4% even less for women's migration. The higher importance of environmental reasons for Senegalese migration could be due to the lower annual average rainfall in the area compared to the Malian study area. The annual average rainfall is 400 mm in the Senegalese study area and thus approximately 100 mm lower than in the Malian study area. This can make a huge difference with respect to people's food security situation.

While environmental reasons are highly intertwined with economic reasons in Senegal, migration motives related to economic reasons in Mali were mainly related to consumption, such as "buying clothes" (45%), "dowry" (28%), "tax" (24%) and "tradition" (11%). Surprisingly, farmers only slightly more often agree to economic migration reasons (71% versus 59%) than people with non-agriculture activities, with no differences for environmental reasons.

Age and the level of education have a considerable effect on the impact of environmental factors on migration. The young and the higher educated people are less likely to migrate for environmental reasons. The youngest people surveyed (18 to 30 years old) migrated less often for environmental reasons than older migrants. Only 7% of young Senegalese migrants indicate food security as their main migration motive, compared to 30% in each of the two older age groups (31 to 50 years old, and 51 years and older). People who were between 31 to 50 years old at migration were the most likely to migrate for environmental

Table 4.1 People's economic and environmental migration motives by country.

Migration motives		Country		Total (n = 1336)
		Senegal (n = 649)	Mali (n = 687)	
Economic reasons as main	n	372	484	856
motive	%	58	71	65
- thereof: economic reasons	n	106	421	527
with no environmental impact	%	29	87	62
- thereof: economic reasons	n	266	63	329
with environmental impact	%	71	13	38
Environmental reasons as	n	292	70	362
main or secondary motive	%	45	10	27

Source: Author.
Migration dataset.

reasons at 38%, compared to those younger than 18 years (21%), those 18 to 30 years old (27%) and those 51 years and older (36%)). Instead, young migrants more often migrated for reasons such as: "visits", "dowry" and "education/vocational training" as main motives and "buying clothes", "adventure/curiosity" and "dowry" as secondary migration motives than older survey participants.

People with a secondary education or a university level hardly migrate for environmental reasons. In Senegal, "food security" played a much bigger role for participants with no formal education (50%) or primary education level (49%) than for those with a high level of education (16%). In Mali, people with all levels of education hardly attribute their migrations to "food security." In both countries, people with a high level of education tend to migrate for education and/or vocational training (55%), while this hardly applies to migrants with primary education (9%) or no formal education (6%). Age, gender and education are important determinants of the migration motives and indicate whose migration is the most likely to be affected by environmental factors. According to the findings, the migration of middle-aged men without formal education or a low level of education is most likely to be driven by environmental stressors.

Changing migration patterns in response to environmental stress

Migration as a response to environmental stress is commonly viewed in literature to be short-term and short-distance migration. Migration from both rural areas in Mali and Senegal related to environmental stressors is mainly short-term, but in contrast to most literature, not necessarily short-distance. Migration patterns from rural Mali and Senegal strongly depend on the migration motives. People who moved from the two rural study areas due to environmental reasons were much more likely to migrate for a short-term period of less than 10 months (59%), than temporarily (24%) or permanently (five years and longer) (18%). Migrants who left for economic reasons stayed equally for a short-term (47%) or a temporary period (47%). In contrast, those who migrated for family reasons – including marriage – were the most likely to migrate permanently. Moreover, farmers were more likely to migrate for a shorter period of time than non-farmers, but only in Mali, which suggests that migration is a complementary activity to agriculture.

In times of stress, people from both rural areas respond to poor rainfall and crop yields either by leaving the home area earlier or by staying longer in migration. Another response to acute environmental stress is to increase the number of migrants within the household or to demand more financial support of those who are already in migration. There has been a significantly higher number of short-term migrations from both rural areas between 1970 and 1979, compared to temporary and permanent migration, and compared to previous and later decades. Short-term migration was also high in Senegal for the most recent migrations between the years 2000 to 2012. Comparing the number of people captured in the survey who migrated in 2010, a year with good rainfall, and in 2011, a year with poor rainfall, the number of migrations was higher for the year 2011 than for 2010. In Senegal, the number of migrations almost doubled from 27 in 2010 to 47 in 2011, and was also higher in Mali in 2011 (69) than in 2010 (54) – a year in which the number had already been high. The percentage of people who indicated "food security" as a migration motive for their migration in 2010 and 2011 was similar for both years in Mali, while in Senegal it increased from 37% in 2010 to 45% in 2011. This could be an indication that poor rainfall indeed increases migration and particularly short-term migration. However, the increase in migration cannot clearly be linked to environmental factors but could have been influenced by other determinants.

The relationship between the migration destinations and the migration motives is less clear. People who migrate for environmental stressors stay not necessarily within the region, but also migrate to farther destinations within the country or even to neighbouring countries. In Mali, migration motivated by environmental reasons has been primarily directed to short-distance destinations within the district of Mopti (36%). Surprisingly, destinations outside the country (29%) were also relevant for migrations for environmental reasons. Farmers from Mali were even more likely to migrate to a neighbouring country than non-farmers. Malians who migrated for economic reasons mainly moved towards neighbouring countries (43%) and Bamako, the capital (36%) (see Figure 4.2). Migrations

Figure 4.2 Tour d'Afrique in Bamako, Mali.
Source: Author.

for "family reasons" were related mainly to short-distance destinations (60%). In Senegal, migrations influenced by environmental reasons were mainly (52%) directed to long-distance destinations within the country, other than the capital. The long-distance destinations were also equally important for migration driven by economic (52%) and family reasons (50%). Dakar was another important destination for Senegalese who migrated for environmental (38%) and economic reasons (34%). Short-distance migration took place primarily for family reasons (30%). Traditionally, women from both rural areas move to their husbands' family after marriage, which usually means moving to a neighbouring village.

Economic migration from both rural areas, but surprisingly also migration for environmental reasons, was often directed to farther destinations within a country or to neighbouring countries. This opposes the general view in literature that environmentally induced migration is mainly short-distance and takes place within national borders. Social networks, better employment opportunities and wage disparities between countries encourage people to migrate to farther destinations. These aspects seem to be more important for the choice of destination rather than the financial means to undertake the journey, which can be borrowed from different sources. International migration to Europe or to other destinations outside the African continent is rare from both study areas due to its high costs and risks. Instead, it is related to economic and personal success rather than to an increased economic need caused by environmental changes. It seems therefore very unlikely that future climate and environmental change will encourage many people from the two rural areas to migrate to Europe.

Bibliography

Black, R., Adger, W.N., Arnell, N.W., Dercon, S., Geddes, A. and Thomas, D. 2011 "The effect of environmental change on human migration" *Global Environmental Change*, 21, S3–S11.

Chant, S.H. ed. 1992 *Gender and migration in developing countries*, London, New York: Belhaven Press.

Davies, S. 1996 *Adaptable livelihoods: Coping with food insecurity in the Malian Sahel*, New York: St. Martin's Press; Macmillan Press.

de Haan, A., Brock, K. and Coulibaly, N. 2002 "Migration, livelihoods and institutions: Contrasting patterns of migration in Mali" *Journal of Development Studies*, 38(5), 37–58.

de Haan, L. and Zoomers, A. 2005 "Exploring the frontier of livelihoods research" *Development and Change*, 36(1), 27–47.

Dugbazah, J. 2012 *Gender, livelihoods and migration in Africa*, [S.l.]: Xlibris Corp.

Ellis, F. 2003 *A livelihood approach to migration and poverty reduction*, UK Department for International Development.

Ezra, M. and Kiros, G.-E. 2001 "Rural out-migration in the drought prone areas of Ethiopia: A multilevel analysis" *International Migration Review*, 35(3), 749–771.

Faist, T. ed. 2013 *Disentangling migration and climate change: Methodologies, political discourses and human rights*, Dordrecht, The Netherlands: Springer.

Findley, S.E. 1994 "Does drought increase migration? A study of migration from rural Mali during the 1983–1985 drought" *International Migration Review*, 28(3), 539–553.

Henry, S., Schoumaker, B. and Beauchemin, C. 2004 "The impact of rainfall on the first out-migration: A multi-level event-history analysis in Burkina Faso" *Population and Environment*, 25(5), 423–460.

Hertrich, V. and Lesclingand, M. 2013 "Adolescent migration in rural Africa as a challenge to gender and intergenerational relationships: evidence from Mali" *The ANNALS of the American Academy of Political and Social Science*, 648(1), 175–188.

Hummel, D., Doevenspeck, M. and Samimi, C. 2012 *Climate change, environment and migration in the Sahel: Selected issues with a focus on Mali and Senegal* (micle – Working Paper 1), Frankfurt am Main: Institute for Social-Ecological Research (ISOE).

Laczko, F. and Aghazarm, C. 2009 *Migration, environment and climate change: Assessing the evidence*, Geneva: International Organization for Migration (IOM).

McLeman, R.A. 2014 *Climate and human migration: Past experiences, future challenges*, New York: Cambridge University Press.

Piguet, E., Pécoud, A. and Guchteneire, P.F.A. de eds. 2011 *Migration and climate change*, Cambridge: Cambridge University Press.

5 The migration decision
Capabilities matter

Migration: not always a strategic household decision

Out-migration from areas affected by environmental stress is considered a strategic household decision to diversify the household's income sources in order to adapt to actual and future environmental stress. Critics of the household approaches, however, have argued since the 1990s that the focus on households neglects intra-household dynamics and unequal power relations within a household or a community. With respect to migration, the power to decide differs between household members along varying characteristics, such as age and gender. Members with less power might therefore either be put under pressure to migrate or be excluded from migration.

In the two rural areas around Bandiagara and Linguère, people's decision to migrate for the first time was often not a household decision. About one-third (36%) of the migrants indicate that nobody had influenced their decision to migrate for the first time. In Mali, half of the male migrants and still 34% of the female migrants decided to migrate by themselves. In Senegal, migration was an individual choice for 39% of the men and only 8% of the women (see Table 5.1). The high share of people migrating based on an individual decision suggests that migration from rural areas affected by environmental changes is not always a household decision. Surprisingly, the migration of farmers and migration for environmental reasons was primarily an individual decision. Farmers more often decided individually about their migration (44%) than people did with another non-agricultural economic activity (28%) in both countries. In Senegal, the majority (64%) of migrants who made the decision by themselves migrated for environmental reasons, while this applies to only 34% of those who consulted father and/or mother. This is surprising because one would assume that people who migrate to support the household's food security and livelihoods discuss their decision to migrate with other household members.

Nevertheless, in Senegal, half of the migrants consulted their father and/or mother about their migration plans, while this applies to 37% of Malians. In the tradition of both societies, young men usually consult their fathers while young women consult their mothers about their decision to migrate. Other family members, such as brothers and sisters, aunts and uncles and friends also influenced the

Table 5.1 Persons who most influenced people's first migration decision by country and gender (shares in percent).

Person who most influenced the first decision to migrate	Country					
	Senegal			Mali		
	Men (n = 211)	Women (n = 170)	Total (n = 381)	Men (n = 267)	Women (n = 130)	Total (n = 397)
Decision influenced by:	61	92	75	49	66	54
- Father and/or mother	50	49	50	33	47	37
- Partner	1	37	17	0	12	4
- Others	10	6	8	16	7	13
Individual decision	39	8	25	51	34	46

Source: Author.

migration decision in Senegal, while friends more often than family members influenced the decision of Malians. The interviews illustrate that there are differences in the degree of influence of other household members. Some young migrants consulted their parents or the household before leaving in order to get their permission, advice or money for the transport. Others only informed their parents and other family members after having made the decision by themselves. Again, other young migrants left without telling anybody beforehand.

Women's first migration is often determined by their partners as indicated by 37% of the Senegalese female migrants, but only for 12% of the Malians. On the contrary, women hardly influenced the migration of their male partners, showing that gender has a considerable effect on the migration decision with women holding less power than men. Men, and particularly the head of the household, make the decisions related to migration which is why female migration in the past has been primarily considered as co-migration with their husbands (David 1995; Petit 1997). The traditional perceptions of social gender roles and a negative social image of independent female migrants in West Africa determine the migration decision of women in a negative way (e.g. Findley 1994; Hertrich and Lesclingand 2013; Sow et al. 2014). Nevertheless, in recent years (2000–12) female migration as an individual decision has shown to be more important in Mali compared to earlier decades. This may be due to a growing need or desire among Malian women to migrate.

The individual migration decision of both men and women is often not a choice but a necessity to uphold traditional hierarchies, particularly when it opposes the will of the household or the community. In the West African Sahel, usually the male head of household decides over the migration of other household members. The unequal distribution of power, with the head of the household as the most powerful decision maker, makes migration (or staying) against the head of the household will almost impossible. That is why young people, both men and women, often migrate secretly and prefer not to talk to their parents or other family members about their migration plans. Migrating against the expressed will of the father is considered a serious affront, and thus much worse than leaving without informing anybody. By leaving secretly, they elude the influence of the traditional authority of the parents, other household members or the community. Young women sometimes inform their mothers about their plans to migrate, forming a secret alliance against the head of the household as the following citation of Oumu, a young Dogon woman, illustrates:

> I left secretly, but I told my mother about my plan. (. . .) In general, it is better not to talk to you father about it because when he refuses and you leave despite his objection, you will find bad luck. (. . .) Some do talk to their mothers beforehand; others tell nobody. (. . .) In general, our mothers will look for money to cover the transport. That is why many people will tell their mothers.
> (Oumu/22 years/female/Mali)

Parents (father, mother or both) who agree to the decision of the young people to migrate often take care of the transport costs and provide their sons or daughters with money and advice. When young people migrate secretly, they often do not have the necessary financial means for the journey. Several interviewees, male and female, admitted to have stolen money from the parents' pockets to be able to pay for the transport.

Migration from areas affected by environmental stress is not always a strategic household decision for the economic benefit of the household. Traditional gender roles and unequal power relations along gender and age – in addition to environmental stress – determine the migration decision and the level of choice of the decision to stay or to migrate. For many young people, migration is an individual decision and often does not correspond with the will of the head of the household, but rather constitutes a rebellion against traditional hierarchies and norms. However, not everybody has the capability or the courage to rebel against existing hierarchies and norms.

Staying: trap or choice?

Populations who do not have the ability to move away from areas affected by environmental stress have more recently gained increased focus and attention in environment-migration research. They have been labelled "trapped populations" and are considered the most vulnerable to environmental change (Black et al. 2011; Foresight 2011; Black and Collyer 2014). Money and social networks influence the migration decision. Therefore, poor people are often assumed not to be able to afford migration in order to adapt to environmental changes (Waddington and Sabates-Wheeler 2003; Van Hear 2004; Fall and

Cissé 2013). In effect, only a few studies consider people's reasons to stay or not and the level of voluntariness in the decision. Knowing that migration from both rural areas is a common phenomenon raises not only the question for the migration reasons, but also the question for the reasons to stay. In the West African Sahel, staying deviates from the norm to migrate, therefore, it seems even more obvious to ask who stays and why. In order to assess whether people are "trapped" in an area affected by environmental stress, it is important to distinguish whether people want or need to stay.

People from the two rural areas in Mali and Senegal assess migration predominantly as positive. Nevertheless, people mention negative aspects of migration in the interviews, including being far away from the family, experiencing difficult living and working conditions and having to adapt to different habits and environments. These reasons may deter people from migrating. Still, most people from both rural areas have personal migration experience. Only 112 people or 19% of the rural survey participants had never left the study areas for three months or longer.

People's reasons to stay in their home community are manifold and imply different levels of choice. The main reasons to stay differ considerably between the two study areas. Most of the Senegalese (57%) stay because they have a lot of work or a relevant position at home. The relevant positions included "village chief," a religious position (e.g. Imam) or other positions with importance for the village such as employees of health centres or teachers. In contrast, Malians (40%) mainly stay because parents or the village community do/does not agree with them leaving the area (see Table 5.2). In Senegal, staying as a result of a lot of work and a relevant position suggests a decision of choice, whereas migration in Mali is for many not an option due to restrictions of the household or the community. Another important motive to stay in both areas is responsibility within

Table 5.2 People's motives for staying by country.

Reasons to stay	Country			
	Senegal (n = 72)		Mali (n = 47)	
	n	%	n	%
Family responsibility (take care of parents; only son/daughter)	20	31	15	32
Did not want to leave	19	29	9	19
Never thought about leaving	16	25	14	30
Work or activity in the areas (a lot of work to do here, relevant position)	27	57	4	8
No migration culture in family	15	23	10	21
Parents or village community does not agree	14	22	19	40
Other	18	28	12	26

Source: Author.
Multiple answers possible.

the family (31% for Senegalese versus 32% for Malians). Reasons to stay such as "family responsibilities" and "no migration culture" may indicate an involuntary or a voluntary character of staying depending on people's situations and preferences. In contrast, reasons as "did not want to leave" and "never thought about leaving", relevant to both study areas, imply more of a voluntary character. "Never thought about leaving" is the only motive more relevant for people who do not depend on agriculture (39%) versus farmers (18%), suggesting that people with year-round employment outside the agricultural sector may not have to think about migration.

Surprisingly, only very few people – all four from Senegal – indicate not having enough money to leave and thus have been included in the category "other." This contrasts with the current narratives in the environment-migration nexus literature that poor people are often not able to afford migration. Rather, it suggests that the financial situation does not play an important role in the decision to migrate and that people who stay in the two rural areas are not very likely to be "trapped" by environmental stress. On the contrary, the interviews show that people will borrow or even steal money for transportation in order to realise migration, if necessary.

The reasons to stay in the home community and their degree of voluntariness differ considerably between men and women. Traditional social norms that may restrict the choice to stay for men also restrict the choice to migrate for women. The main reasons for men to stay relate to choice and voluntary action rather than a need to stay. Reasons such as a lot of work to do or having a relevant position in the village enable them to stay and constitute a socially accepted reason not to migrate. In contrast, women in both rural areas often do not have the ability to choose between migrating and staying. At best, they simply have no migration culture (28% in both areas) or never thought about leaving (28% in Senegal versus 37% in Mali). Migration culture among men facilitates their migration, while at the same time, staying might require a justification. For women, it is the opposite case. Since the independent migration of women is a more recent phenomenon, they have to justify migrating rather than staying. In particular, women that belong to the Fulani and Dogon ethnicities often do not have a tradition in labour migration. Despite lacking a migration tradition, some women seem to want to migrate but face restrictions in doing so. A high share of women stays because the parents and village community do not agree with their decision to migrate (34% for Senegalese women and 46% for Malians).

Social norms, often shaped by the unequal power relations by age and gender, play an important role in the decision to migrate or to stay for women and men. The independent labour migration of young women does not match with the traditional role of young women in the rural areas. They are expected to stay at the side of their mothers and help them with their daily tasks. Therefore, female migration still has a negative social image and is often not desired and accepted by many males. The migration of married women is, in both areas, very uncommon for traditional reasons and requires the permission of their husbands. It is thus not surprising that women in the survey were on average younger than their male counterparts at their last reported migration (27 years for women versus 33 years for men).

In Senegal, the migration of young women seems to be fairly accepted whereas in Mali, young women still face heavy constraints to migrate. In some Malian villages, male community members impose sanctions to prevent young women from leaving the village and to enforce their traditional role. Actions to discourage young women from migrating and punishing them for doing so include enforcing high monetary fines to the girls' families in the case of migration and bribing the border posts to restrict the passage of unmarried girls or to put them into prison to frighten them. Moreover, brothers or other male community members are charged to find girls in migration and force them back to the village. These measures are justified by arguing that they will protect the young girls from the dangers in the cities due to their "vulnerable nature". Male villagers argue that these sanctions prevent the problems and shame that female migrants can pose on the family or the village in case the traditionally espoused women return pregnant or with a child. Women in these villages do not have the same capabilities to choose between migrating and staying as men, or as women from other areas who do not face restrictions to their migration decision.

Some young women may favour staying in the village; however, compared to other household or community members, they do not have the capability to decide whether to migrate or not. Many young women do not agree with the restrictions imposed by the parents and/or the village community that prevent them from leaving as illustrated in the following citation by Fatima, a young Malian woman:

> They cannot prohibit us to leave. The girls have to go to Bamako to earn money and to return because in the village there are months where there is nothing to do. There are no jobs here. It is not good to retain us at home.
>
> (Fatima/22 years/ female/Mali)

While many young women stay in the villages because they fear the consequences of their action, others migrate secretly. This might explain the higher share of migration as individual decision among the Dogon women compared to the Senegalese. The secret escape of young women constitutes a rebellion against the imposed sanctions and against the narrow traditional patriarchal norms of both societies. For the young Dogon women, Petit had already suggested in the 1990s that labour migration had become "a sign of protest against the authority of the elders " [translated by author, original: "un signe de contestation envers l'autorité des aînés"] (Petit 1997: 539). The labour migration of women, notes Petit, endangers the continuation of the hierarchies between gender and age and the domination of men over women and elderly over the younger members in a family (Petit 1997: 539).

The migration of some young women despite heavy constraints may eventually contribute to ease the restrictions against female migration and lead to a higher acceptance of their migration. Some villages already abolished the ban against female migration and "liberated" women from the restrictions because it did not prevent them from leaving. Village elders justify the lifting of the ban by explaining that women now needed to migrate due to a lack of financial means. Whether there is a greater need to migrate or not, young female labour migrants – especially those who migrate secretly – are particularly at risk because they usually do not rely on social networks and have little (financial) support to find a place to stay and work. They are thus easy targets for crimes, such as exploitation and sexual abuse, in the destination areas.

Migration: a necessity and/or an opportunity

People living in an area affected by environmental changes are usually not equally vulnerable to environmental stressors because the stressors often aggravate already existing vulnerabilities, such as poverty (Blaikie 1994; Kliot 2004; IOM 2009). The ability to migrate and to adapt to environmental stress depends on the local social-ecological context and people's assets. The social-ecological context may include the availability and quality of the local employment opportunities, the conditions for harvests, the development of infrastructure in the region, the number of working age (male) household members and social norms. People's assets for migrating and adapting to environmental stress include, among others, social networks, education, skills, health, the quantity and quality of land and livestock and the amount of money available.

If alternative local employment opportunities are rare and environmental stress endangers the household's food security, migration may be a last resort. To describe this type of migration as an adaptation strategy to environmental changes would be euphemistic because adaptation implies a certain form of agency (Bakewell 2010). Migration as a last resort, however, implies that people do not have the capability to decide between migrating and staying, but are forced to leave. From the two rural areas, only very few interviewees indicated having no other choice but to migrate in order to ensure their own and their family's food security. Migration was primarily a last resort for people who migrated during the severe droughts in the 1970s or 1980s. Ndaga, a middle-aged Senegalese man living in Dakar, reflects on his need to leave the study area in 1983. His experience highlights that people who lack financial means prefer to borrow money for transport in order to try to make a living elsewhere rather than to stay in the rural areas and to accept their fate.

> I had no money to stay there, in the village. (. . .) I took the decision to be the first to leave because I had nothing left; I had no means at all that would allow me to stay . . . Somebody lent me the money for the transport to Dakar.
> (Ndaga/55 years/male/Senegal)

Elderly people, in particular, repeatedly recall the devastating consequences of the extreme droughts in the 1970s and 1980s with respect to the impact of environmental stress on their livelihoods. In contrast, recent environmental stressors seemed to be perceived as less important. Although people feel that the climate and environmental conditions alongside the outcome of the yields are not much better than in earlier times, the effect of repeatedly poor rainfalls on people's livelihoods are much less devastating. This is primarily due to better adaptation strategies that have been developed over the last decades including the diversification of income within a household.

Nevertheless, even today, migration is not a free choice for everybody. People who really need to leave the rural areas are usually stricken by a combination of environmental stress, a high dependence on farming, little assets (e.g. no education) and unfavourable social conditions (e.g. no other male members in the household). Often, they are among the poorest in the community. Moussa's case (see Box 5.1) highlights that an unfavourable household composition as the only male family member combined with poor conditions for agriculture can generate an urgent need to leave the rural areas and find alternative employment elsewhere. Large households with several working age men can more easily adapt to the absence of migrants and may allow other members to stay. However, the effect of a young man's absence can be particularly harsh on smaller households. While David (1995) found 20 years ago that receiving remittances was considered a poor substitute for the young man's labour force on the field in central Mali, Moussa's case and other interviewees suggest that nowadays the migrant's remittances more than compensate for the loss of labour. Today families often prefer to send one or several male household members to the city in order to receive more remittances that allow for a better living standard. At the same time, they either reduce the work in agriculture or distribute it among a lower number of people. Nowadays, migration as a last resort is more of an exception in both rural areas.

Box 5.1   Moussa

Moussa, a 30-year-old man from rural Senegal, had few options to stay in the village even though he wanted to. Moussa is the only son in the family and therefore, he became responsible for the food security of his mother and sister after his father had died. For several years, he continued cultivating rain-fed crops with his mother and sister during the rainy season in the village and migrated to work in Dakar for about five months during the dry season. Insufficient yields due to lack of rain and lack of farming equipment, combined with the uncertainty and unreliability of satisfying yields, led to Moussa's decision to find a more reliable employment elsewhere. The labour migration to Dakar seemed to be his only option to ensure the family's livelihood, although he would have preferred to stay in the village and gain his living as a farmer. Today, Moussa works as a mechanic assistant in Dakar and only returns to the village to visit his family. Moussa never went to school, which restricts his options to low-paid employment.

Nevertheless, even low-paid employment seems more profitable and reliable than farming. His mother and sister continue farming by themselves for their living and Moussa supports them with cash he earns in Dakar. His financial support not only ensures the household's food security, but also allows his mother and sister to remain unconcerned in the village.

> Farming does not work as well as it should. There are many obstacles, mainly related to the availability of farming equipment and rain. (. . .) It is logical that you don't continue an activity that is not useful. You have to look for an alternative employment, something else to do. If all our hopes rest on agriculture, we are obliged to cultivate during the rainy season and to hope every time for improvement. (. . .) If everything turned out as good as we had hoped, we would by far prefer to stay in the village and only leave for a short time to work and then return to the village. (. . .) The rainy season is not what it used to be as rainfall has decreased. We have cultivated but without yield. We have to struggle and to work hard in order to maintain the livelihood of our family. Leaving the village is the only alternative.

Even though migration may not be a last resort in most cases, some people, particularly men, may not have the freedom to choose to stay due to social pressure. Men are traditionally the breadwinners for the household and have to ensure the household's food security either through local activities or through migration. Young men are expected to contribute to the household's income and to increase the economic situation of the family. The first-born son, in particular, has a traditional obligation to contribute to the household's livelihoods and to meet the expectations of the parents. Moreover, the migration of boys is also considered an important part of the transition to manhood and often a common habit among peers. Usually many other men of the community, the peer group and the household have migrated before which in addition increases the pressure to migrate for young men. If most friends, neighbours and brothers migrate, young men usually do not have the capability to choose to stay as an option. Those who refuse to migrate in the two rural areas because they do not want to leave face mockery by friends and are perceived as lazy by the household and village community. Therefore, the pressure on men to migrate is present in both rural areas and is independent from the environmental conditions and the quality of yields. Local employment opportunities are rare around Bandiagara and Linguère and agriculture only demands high labour during the three-month rainy season. This leaves migration often as the only available means to diversify the income and ensure the household's food security.

Migration motives, pattern and the need to migrate also change with a person's marital status and the respective responsibility for a household. Married women generally no longer migrate as they are usually expected to take care of the household and the children. Particularly for men, the need to migrate to ensure the family's food security increases as a result of having a family, as the case of Elhadj illustrates (see Box 5.2). In Senegal, only one-fourth of the singles migrated for food security reasons, while half of the married people migrated for environmental reasons with only a slight difference between monogamous and polygamous married respondents. In Mali, the survey shows similar results; however, the general agreement to food security as a migration motive was much lower than in Senegal.

Box 5.2   Elhadj

Elhadj is a 60-year-old man with three grown-up children from the rural area of Linguère. Farming is his main economic activity, but he complements it with gains from migration. Every dry season, he migrates to Dakar for two to four months to work at the fish market and then returns to the rural area for the rainy season. For the most part of the year, he stays in the village with his family. The quality of the yields may influence the duration of his stay in Dakar but does not influence the migration itself.

Elhadj's case demonstrates how the need to migrate increases for men when starting a family. His reasons for migration changed after marriage and with the start of a family. As an unmarried young man, Elhadj migrated for adventure and a desire for modern goods. The money he gained in migration was only spent for himself in order to fulfil his own needs and desires. Since the start of his family, however, he migrates to fulfil the needs of his own household and those of his parents. Thus, migration became a necessity to ensure the family's food security and well-being after his marriage.

> It has been a long time since I first left my village. I was about 15 years old and went to Dakar. It was a decision of a young man and I was not motivated by a lot of things. (. . .) It is often popular to leave, to make an effort, to be able to buy trousers or a shirt for yourself. It has been a basic education for me and it was also hip to leave. (. . .) We left for adventure, to see what's going on. (. . .) Now I am responsible, I am proud of my life. (. . .) I started to notice that leaving was a necessity after having founded a family. Everything I earn, I divided it into two parts: one for my parents and the rest for my family. Earlier, everything I earned was for my daily activities, but since I have a wife, it's a necessity to leave for work and to satisfy needs.

Elhadj continues to migrate each year even at his relatively old age because his children study and cannot replace him. He prefers to migrate in order to finance the education of his children, which he hopes will allow them a better life in the future.

Migration from the rural areas may be influenced by a certain need to migrate for some people; the majority of the people from the rural areas in Mali and Senegal, however, assess temporary migration as very positive. The vast majority of people (86%) would advise other family members to migrate, although 25% thereof would limit this advice to migration within the country or the continent. The positive assessment of migration in the two rural areas suggests that migration constitutes an opportunity rather than a necessity, based on a voluntary decision. For 85% of respondents from Mali and Senegal, the financial support of migrants from their families is an advantage of migration. Other advantages of migration cited include "to learn new things" for 80% in Senegal and 43% in Mali, "returning with new ideas and experience" for 57% of Senegalese and 32% of Malians, "buying clothes" for 41% of Senegalese and 50% of Malians and "learning languages" for 22% of Senegalese and 33% of Malians. The emancipation of young women and the independence from the family were other advantages of migration indicated by the respondents.

In the qualitative interviews, both men and women highlight that migration benefits the household and the migrant. Economic advantages mentioned include gaining money to support the family or to invest in housing, agriculture and/or other businesses, being able to save money and to afford consumer goods, such as clothing, jewellery, a motorcycle or a mobile phone. People, however, not only emphasise the economic advantages of migration, but also point to personal gains, such as learning new languages, getting to know new people, improving skills or even discovering new things and behaviours. In general, interviewees portray migration as a means to discover the world outside the village, to getting "civilised," and as an "école de vie" [school of life, author].

For many people, migration is both a necessity and an opportunity at the same time. Although the financial support of the migrant members is crucial for most households in the rural areas, for many it is not the main reason for migration. Instead, the migration – particularly of young people – is often motivated by both individual motives and the need to contribute to the household's livelihood. The variety of advantages mentioned for migration and the different migration reasons suggest that migration is often an opportunity and a necessity. Baba Yatta, an elderly man from Senegal, suggests that economic independence and the acquisition of consumer goods are important motives for young people to leave, alongside with the necessity of providing financial support.

> Necessity only has meaning as long as it is continuous. There is an appeal at a certain age for goods. It feels good to have them when you are young. If not we would leave from here.
>
> (Baba Yatta/70 years/male/Senegal)

He further highlights the economic and non-economic benefits of migration for young people, explaining why migration takes place independently from the yields:

> Yes, when the yields are good, some stay and others leave nevertheless. (. . .) This is important because, even if you do not earn anything during

your journey, you will still learn new things. Some young people therefore
leave in order to take the opportunity to learn something.

(Baba Yatta/70 years/male/Senegal)

This illustrates that the reasons for migration are more often related to opportunities rather than a need to leave. As livelihood studies suggest, migration is
not only part of a coping strategy to external – including environmental – stress
but also a means of expanding a household's livelihoods and to accumulate assets
(Ellis 2003; UNDP 2009). Thereby, migration constitutes an opportunity for the
household and for the migrant herself/himself. The lack of local employment
in both areas encourages migration, but people often prefer to migrate even if
there are local employment opportunities, due to expected higher gains from
labour activity elsewhere. Development projects in several villages in both rural
areas aim at reducing the need to migrate by creating off-seasonal employment
opportunities, such as working in vegetable gardens or vast irrigated fields. These
projects might reduce the need to migrate for those who prefer to stay, but do not
detract people from leaving. Many people migrate despite the additional income
opportunities on-site because opportunities elsewhere are often (presumed to be)
better. Seydou and his brother explain why. The brothers originate from a Malian
village surrounded by huge irrigated fields, but prefer to work as a cook and a
waiter in a hotel in Bamako. The main reason they left was that the economic
gains from the employment at the hotel were higher than what they could get
from the irrigated gardening.

If you leave or not depends on the amount of money you earn. (. . .) Since
there is this dam [for irrigating fields, author] in the village, people stay. (. . .)
We are here in Bamako because we earn more in Bamako than in the village.

(Seydou/45 years/male/Mali)

Another indicator for the voluntary and temporary character of most people's
migration is that people in both Mali and Senegal are optimistic about the future
of their villages. When asked about future projections on the development of the
village over the next five years, people are mainly positive. In Mali, 85% of the
survey participants think that the village will continue to develop, 5% believe
it will not change and 10% think the conditions will worsen. In Senegal, people
are more sceptical about the development of their village with 65% perceiving
that the village will continue to develop in the next five years, 15% believe it will
not change and 20% think it may worsen. In general, migrants interviewed in the
capitals were slightly more optimistic about the future of their villages than the
rural population themselves.

When asked if people wanted the government to act in order to influence
migration, most wished for the government to support migration. Half of the people would like the government to encourage or to facilitate migration while 26%
thought that the government should reduce migration. Another 15% wanted the
government to prevent migration while only 3% did not want the government

to act. The remaining had no opinion on the issue. The high level of agreement on encouraging or facilitating mobility suggests that migration is not just a response to unfavourable living conditions but also a means to realise opportunities. Particularly the migration of young and well-educated people has a voluntary character, linked to individual motives rather than to household needs. As a result, government policies and development activities should focus on facilitating migration in the respective countries as well as the broader West African sub-region, instead of trying to reduce or prevent migration.

Household's needs as justification for migration

Earlier studies on migration, livelihoods and environmental change suggest that people use fulfilling households' needs as reason to justify migration even if migration may take place for other reasons. Gonin and Lassailly-Jacob (2002) explain in their study on environmental refugees that migration used to be a necessary strategy to cope with the severe droughts of the 1970s and 1980s, but that environmental reasons have become an excuse for migration since the 1990s. Despite the possibility to work in agriculture, migrants would prefer to migrate and to imitate the success of previous migrants (Gonin and Lassailly-Jacob 2002: 13). Moreover, Davies (1996) shows in her study on adaptable livelihoods and food security in Mali that "there was little evidence of these decisions being driven primarily by the need to leave in order to reduce household consumption, although this was cited as an important contributory justification" (Davies 1996: 75). Instead diverse opportunities and individual whims motivated people's migration.

Interviewees from the two study areas in Mali and Senegal tend to indicate the household's need as a main impetus for migration. Reasons related to the household's need, such as lack of money or food or supporting the household, are socially accepted. However, further along in the interview, young people attribute their desire to migrate for more individual reasons, such as curiosity or their own economic desires. These migration motives are often not very well-respected in the community or accepted within the household. Moreover, the social expectations with respect to migration differ among men and women and influence the given reasons for migration. The migration of young men is well-established in both societies. Men are even expected to migrate in order to contribute to the household's income and thus do not have to give a specific migration motive or justify their migration. Quite the contrary, they have to justify their stay rather than their migration. The interviews suggest, however that their migration motives are often encouraged by individual aspirations rather than by household's needs.

Labour migration of women in contrast is not well-established. Women therefore have to justify their migration. Young unmarried women from Mali mostly indicated in the interviews that today, in contrast to earlier times, they have to migrate due to a lack of financial means in order to prepare for their marriage. This seems to correspond with the survey results in which economic motives were the main driver of the migration of men and surprisingly also for women from both rural areas. This finding, however, contrasts with earlier studies on female migration from rural Mali that found no or very little (less than 10%) agreement to economic reasons for women's migration (Findley 1994; Petit 1997) and suggests that migration motives have changed over time for women. Indeed, particularly young women from Mali (the 18- to 30-year-olds) more often stated economic reasons, such as "dowry" and "buying clothes," as their main motive for migrating than older age groups. At the same time, the importance of family reasons for migration has decreased for young Malian women. The changes of migration motives among Malian women could either point to an increasing need or desire for cash compared to earlier times.

The interviews and further inquiry, however, suggest that the lack of means and preparation for marriage are socially accepted reasons often used to justify migration motivated by other less accepted reasons. The variety of such hidden migration motives is broad and includes not only economic aspects, such as gaining financial independence and being able to afford consumer goods, but also non-economic aspects related to life experiences, such as learning new skills, experiencing city life and discovering new things outside of the village. Hidden migration motives also include aspects that oppose traditional social norms, such as gaining a greater autonomy, realising a love marriage or postponing an arranged marriage – like in the case for Binta (see Box 5.3).

Box 5.3   Binta

Binta, a 22-year-old unmarried woman from rural Mali, first left the village at age 14 for Bamako. First, she stayed for three months working as a housemaid and after returning to the village, she migrated again, once for two years and the next time for another four years. In the interview, Binta stated that migration is a necessity for young women to be able to cover their basic needs and to prepare for their marriage. Against the usual practice of individual interviews, the interview with Binta had to take place in the presence of her father and other male community members. It is thus not surprising that she did not admit her actual migration motives, but would give a rather socially accepted reason to explain the need of her migration. Further individual talks with Binta and other family members, however, suggest that Binta actually migrates for other reasons. One main reason is to escape from her marriage. Her parents had arranged the marriage with the son of a befriended family when she was six years old – as it is still tradition among the Dogon. Today, her future husband is a known alcoholic and is already married to three other women. At the same time, Binta has two little children from a man she got to know in Bamako and whom she would prefer to marry. The reason she cannot do this is that she does not have her parent's permission due to the earlier marriage arrangements and the shame for the family to renege the promise. Against Binta's initial statement, it seems very unlikely that she migrates to prepare for a marriage she strongly opposes. Migrating to join the father of her children, in contrast seems to be a more obvious – but not socially accepted – migration motive. Moreover, Binta likes to live in the city very much. She appreciates being able to afford new clothes and goods due to her paid work and that she learned Bambara, a main local language in Mali. Although Binta's father and the male villagers do not want her and other women to migrate, Binta has escaped secretly several times already in order to live and work in Bamako.

The ability to earn money, instead of relying on their mother's or future husband's financial aid, is a particularly important aspect of female migration. It leads not only to social prestige and acceptance among peers but also to greater autonomy and empowerment of young women. Young women spend most of the money gained in migration on goods, such as fashionable clothes, jewellery, mobile phones and kitchen equipment, for themselves but also for family and friends. The women's ability to earn their own money and to afford consumer goods that they can bring back to the village gives them a sense of pride, and at the same time, increases their prestige and social standing among friends and in the community. It also makes them a better candidate for marriage. Moreover, it challenges traditional social norms that favour the traditional role of men as breadwinners of the household and women as caretakers of the housework and the children. The traditional gender roles also imply a high financial dependency of women on male household members. The independent migration of young women and young men contributes to changes in the daily life and social norms back in the village.

The findings show that not all migrants support the household financially, which suggests that many young men migrate as a result of individual motives rather than household needs. The main disadvantages of migration for 36% of Senegalese and 31% of Malians were that "migrants do not send money" and "the lack of labour force." Further disadvantages mentioned were that "migrants come back with bad ideas and behaviour" for 34% of Senegalese and 19% of Malians and that they "lack respect of traditions" (31% versus 16%). Another less important disadvantage mentioned was the "change of language and appearances" of the migrants. These disadvantages indicate a certain fear of change of the traditional social norms in the villages. For Malians, the pregnancy of young migrant women was a major concern for 41% compared to 17% in Senegal.

Binta's case and the interviews of other young women suggest that the need to migrate due to a lack of financial means to prepare for marriage seems to be a silent social agreement between men and women in the Dogon country to justify the undesirable migration of young women. It seems to be a compromise by which the male community and household members can justify the migration of female members without losing face, when noting that the prohibition of female migration is no longer effective. In contrast to women's offensive violation of the ban of female migration, the silent agreement does not undermine the "superior" position of the father and the male elders.

Some years ago, Petit wrote that Dogon women migrate independently in order to "look for a greater autonomy, a liberation from the paternalism of men and elders. This emancipation doubles with the wish to live an easier life enabled through consumer goods, an additional comfort" [translated by author, original: "chercher une autonomie plus grande, un affranchissement de la tutelle des hommes et des aine(e)s. Cette émancipation se double évidemment du souhait d'avoir une vie matérielle plus facile, un confort supplémentaire"] (Petit 1997: 538). Today, Petit's interpretation seems to apply more than ever. In contrast to earlier studies, women relate their independent migration today to economic reasons.

Irrespective of whether the need to prepare for marriage and to gain additional financial means exists or not, migration can constitute an opportunity for young women to expand their capabilities by accumulating assets (financial, social and human capital) in migration. The independent migration of young women contributes to a greater (financial) autonomy and to greater empowerment. Financial autonomy contributes to the ability of women to challenge their low power position compared to men within the household and the community. This has positive effects on women's self-image and status, as has similarly been reported in some studies from rural Mali (Petit 1997; Hertrich and Lesclingand 2012). Just as successful male migration shaped the perception of migration and the image of the successful migrant, women's economic independence and success will likely change traditional gender roles and social norms, unequal power relations in the household and the community, as well as the negative perception of female migration.

Migration under the cover of socially accepted motives, such as contributing to the household income, allows people to realise goals that would otherwise elude them, such as satisfying curiosity, seeking adventure, achieving a different lifestyle, independence from the parents or escaping from narrow social norms. Individual motives and aspirations are important drivers of young people's migration from both rural areas, but may be justified or achieved with the cover of needing to support the household financially. Not all migrations in an area affected by environmental changes can be considered an adaptation strategy or a failure to adapt, but environment-migration research also needs to consider underlying individual migration motives.

What shapes capabilities to migrate and to stay

People in rural Mali and Senegal do have different capabilities with respect to their migration decision. Different structural factors, such as cultural, demographic, economic, environmental and social aspects shape people's capability set with respect to livelihood options and the migration decision. In addition to structural conditions, household and individual characteristics can be decisive in determining people's capabilities and their reasons to stay or to migrate.

Climate stressors and environmental factors do influence people's migration decision and their capabilities to migrate and stay, but often in combination with other structural factors, mostly social aspects. Therefore, these structural drivers can be designated as "social-ecological conditions". The research presented in this book has shown that unfavourable social-ecological conditions force farmers to leave rather than to stay in the village. Moreover, many women – especially in Mali – were forced to stay in the rural areas due to restrictions based on traditional social norms, making them more vulnerable to environmental stressors. In both cases, people did not have the capability to choose.

The social conditions that shape people's capabilities to migrate or to stay are not only social norms, such as gender roles and migration tradition, but are often determined by household characteristics. These include the composition of the household, migration experience within the household, the attitude of the household towards migration and the household's assets or capitals (social networks, financial means etc.). For a female-headed household or households with a low number of men in working age, it is much more difficult to cope with environmental stress and to compensate the lack of labour in agriculture caused by the migration of one or several male household members. Migration experience within the household usually leads to a positive attitude towards migration, making migration for other family members more likely. Assets, such as social networks and financial means, facilitate migration and shape migration patterns.

In addition to household characteristics, individual characteristics influence people's capabilities in their decision to migrate. These include characteristics such as age, economic activity (agriculture or other), formal education, gender and marital status. Young men migrate more often for voluntary reasons such as the desire for consumer goods and for adventure. The reasons and the capabilities to migrate often change after having founded a family. This often increases the need to migrate in order to ensure the family's food security and livelihoods. Women need the permission of their parents and village to leave before marriage and the permission of their husbands after marriage. They thus often cannot choose to migrate, while young men may not have the capability to choose to stay due to social expectations and the culture related to the migration of young men. The well-educated usually migrate for better educational or professional prospects while farmers' migration heavily depends on environmental factors. Farmers often have to and want to migrate seasonally in order to complement their agricultural yields or they have to leave their activity permanently in order to ensure the household's food security.

People's capabilities do not only shape the migration decision and the reasons to leave, but in turn migration reasons can also influence people's capabilities. Migration reasons that imply a need to migrate usually restrain people's capabilities to stay but interestingly, may also increase the capabilities to migrate for those who would not be able to migrate otherwise. For instance, young men and women who claim to migrate in order to support the household financially or to prepare one's marriage, are not likely to face restrictions with respect to their decision to migrate. Individual motives, such as being independent from the parents and postponing or avoiding an arranged marriage, are less accepted migration motives and may incite restrictions with respect to migration. A migration decision, however, is not only influenced by people's capabilities to migrate and stay, but also by people's preferences and aspirations – two aspects that are often neglected in research on migration in developing countries.

Bibliography

Bakewell, O. 2010 "Some reflections on structure and agency in migration theory" *Journal of Ethnic and Migration Studies*, 36(10), 1689–1708.

Black, R., Bennett, S.R.G., Thomas, S.M. and Beddington, J.R. 2011 "Migration as adaptation" *Nature*, 478, 447–449.

Black, R. and Collyer, M. 2014 "Populations 'trapped' at times of crisis" *Forced Migration Review*, 45, 52–56.

Blaikie, P.M. 1994 *At risk: Natural hazards, people's vulnerability, and disasters*, London, New York: Routledge.

David, R. 1995 *Changing places? Women, resource management and migration in the Sahel: Case studies from Senegal, Burkina Faso, Mali and Sudan*, London: SOS Sahel International (UK).

Davies, S. 1996 *Adaptable livelihoods: Coping with food insecurity in the Malian Sahel*, New York: St. Martin's Press; Macmillan Press.

Ellis, F. 2003 *A livelihood approach to migration and poverty reduction*, UK Department for International Development.

Fall, A.S. and Cissé, R. 2013 "Migratory dynamics over half a century in Senegal: A longitudinal perspective over four generations" *International Relations and Diplomacy*, 1(3), 189–201.

Findley, S.E. 1994 "Does drought increase migration? A study of migration from rural Mali during the 1983–1985 drought" *International Migration Review*, 28(3), 539–553.

Foresight 2011 *Migration and global environmental change: Future challenges and opportunities* (Final Project Report), London: The Government Office for Science.

Gonin, P. and Lassailly-Jacob, V. 2002 "Les réfugiés de l'environnement" *Revue européenne des migrations internationales*, 18(2), 139–160.

Hertrich, V. and Lesclingand, M. 2012 "Adolescent migration and the 1990s nuptiality transition in Mali" *Population Studies*, 66(2), 147–166.

Hertrich, V. and Lesclingand, M. 2013 "Adolescent migration in rural Africa as a challenge to gender and intergenerational relationships: Evidence from Mali" *The ANNALS of the American Academy of Political and Social Science*, 648(1), 175–188.

IOM 2009 *Compendium of IOM's activities in migration, climate change and the environment*, Geneva: International Organization for Migration (IOM).

Kliot, N. 2004 "Environmentally induced population movements: Their complex soucres and consequences: A critical review", in Unruh, J.D., Krol, M.S. and Kliot, N. eds. *Environmental change and its implications for population migration*, Dordrecht, The Netherlands: Kluwer Academic Publishers, 69–99.

Petit, V. 1997 "Société d'origine et logiques migratoires: Les Dogon de Sangha (Mali)" *Population (French Edition)*, 52(3), 515–543.

Sow, P., Adaawen, S. and Scheffran, J. 2014 "Migration, social demands and environmental change amongst the Frafra of Northern Ghana and the Biali in Northern Benin" *Sustainability*, 6(1), 375–398.

UNDP 2009 *Human development report 2009. Overcoming barriers: Human mobility and development*, New York: United Nation Development Programme.

Van Hear, N. 2004 *'I went as far as my money would take me': Conflict, forced migration and class* (Working Paper 6), Oxford: Centre on Migration, Policy and Society (COMPAS), University of Oxford.

Waddington, H. and Sabates-Wheeler, R. 2003 *How does poverty affect migration choice: A review of literature* (Working Paper T3), Brighton: Development Research Centre on Migration, Globalisation and Poverty, University of Sussex.

6 Aspirations for a better life

"Faire la jeunesse" – youth migration

In 2006, the UN news service IRIN published an article entitled "Mankind is like this: one wants to get ahead" (IRIN news 2006). The article tells the story of Mansour, an illegal migrant from Senegal who is desperate to migrate to Europe in order to "get ahead". Although Mansour may not originate from an area that is affected by environmental changes, people from such areas also aspire to "get ahead" and give their life value. An increased exposure to information about the outside world by the media that display images from cities or other places of the world, shapes aspirations for a different lifestyle and/or a better future (de Bruijn and van Dijk 2004; Schapendonk 2010). In addition, the success of previous migrants (described in more detail in the next chapter), the narratives and positive image around the migrants and their changed appearance lead to transformations in the rural communities and influence young people's aspirations.

The migration of young men is a common experience in the rural areas of the West African Sahel. Young people from the rural study areas often prefer to migrate in order to discover different parts of their country, the region or the world. They are particularly attracted by urban areas, in which the way of life differs vastly from rural life. "Faire la jeunesse" [in English: "enjoying youth"; author] is the term often used to refer to the migration of young men, particularly in Mali. The term "faire la jeunesse" implies the commonness and popularity of migration for young men for decades and its relevance as a rite of passage in their transition to manhood. Another term to describe the migration of young men is "aller en aventure" [in English: "go on an adventure"; author]. The term already suggests that migration is not just a necessity to fulfil the household's needs, but that it is a voluntary endeavour that reflects individual interests. According to Graw and Schielke, the term *adventure* "emphasizes the ability and decisiveness to act, the will to take risks and to realize oneself, rather than expressing the underlying conditions, vulnerabilities or afflictions" (Graw and Schielke 2012: 32).

Young people's migration motives differ considerably from those of elder respondents. The youngest migrants were less likely to state environmental reasons for their migrations and instead migrated for individual motives, such as education or vocational training, clothes, adventure or visits. Young people often have great aspirations for a better life and a "modern" lifestyle. Life in the rural areas is considered hard and boring and offers little opportunities. Important migration motives for young people are economic independence, curiosity and the acquisition of consumer goods. Economic motives include financial independence to be able to afford fashionable clothes and other consumer goods, to be financially independent from parents, to gain prestige and to be able to live a "modern" lifestyle. Young men and women usually spend a fair amount of money on consumer goods for themselves, friends or other family members. This includes "fashionable" clothing, smart phones, motorcycles and other things that are not available in the rural areas. These things will usually improve their social standing among friends and within the community.

The desire for consumer goods is often strongly influenced by the success of previous migrations of friends, family and community members. The appearance of return migrants, the changes in style (clothing, jewellery, etc.) and the possession of consumer goods of migrants distinguishes them significantly from those who do not migrate, creating inequality among peer groups. This in turn creates aspirations in others to afford a similar lifestyle and encourages both young men and women to migrate, because this seems to be the only feasible way to realise these aspirations. Khady, a young woman and Samba, a man from Senegal explain how the migration of others encourages the migration of young men and women to migrate to the cities:

> There are many girls who go to work in the city, it's "à la mode". (. . .) Those girls who are in Dakar have money and buy equipment, new clothes and aid their families. Those who stay in the village have nothing. (. . .) Therefore, they like to pursue the same path.
>
> (Khady/20 years/female/Senegal)

> My other brothers can't stay because every time I come back to the village I bring things. Things they can't possess while staying in the village.
>
> (Samba/44 years/male/Senegal)

Migration of young people, however, is not only related to economic gains, but also to non-economic goals, such as satisfying curiosity, seeking adventure, meeting people, being more independent from family and village community, as well as gaining experience and learning skills, such as a language, cooking or a profession. The case of Malik (see Box 6.1) highlights that migration arises among young boys as an adventure to "faire la jeunesse" rather than as a response to environmental stress.

Box 6.1   Malik

Malik is a 34-year-old farmer from rural Mali. He never went to school, but helped his parents on the fields. When Malik was 14 years old, he first left the village in order to live and work in Bamako for three years. Encouraged by the narratives of his older brother about the city life of Bamako, he wanted to see for himself what the big city life was like.

> I left because my brother was in Bamako and he had told me about the city because I had never been there. (. . .) He told me about many things, about the big houses and the climate and about how people dress. He said I would have to see that and I did. (. . .) I wanted to get to know the city of Bamako, to get to know a bit and to learn some Bambara [a common local language spoken in Mali, the local language spoken in the study area is Dogon; author].

His migration was driven by the desire to get to know the capital of his country, to experience urban life and to be able to afford consumer goods and clothes – things that differed from what was available in the village and the nearby town. In addition to the goods bought for himself, he also sent money back home to the family.

> My work in Bamako was not great work, I only guarded a house. But with what I earned, I paid clothes and other things for the family and I also sent them some money to pay for food and other things. (. . .) For myself, I bought clothes and a lot of things that are a bit different, things that do not exist in the village.

When Malik talks about his migration experience, his eyes are filled with joy and he speaks passionately, almost a bit nostalgically. It becomes clear that although he financially supported the family with what he earned through migration, his decision to go to Bamako was not driven primarily by household needs. After some years in Bamako – which he enjoyed – he decided to return to the village.

> I went to see, I saw and I was happy. I have earned some money and I returned because it is better in the village. In the city, all you earn, you spend directly, that's why I returned.

Later he left for a vocational training in tourism to Mopti, a nearby city, where he lived and worked for eight years before permanently returning to the village. Now, he prefers to live in the village where he got married and founded a family. Since then, he no longer leaves for longer periods. In the village, he cultivates millet, beans and other crops, but also works as a tour guide and makes "bogolans", handmade Malian cotton fabrics, for sale.

Although for many young people migration is an adventure, it is often also a means to provide financial support to the household as demonstrated by Malik's case. The following citation from a Senegalese man echoes this phenomenon:

> Two things have motivated me to leave, adventure and discovering new things but also the search for employment. (. . .) The livestock breeding was not anymore sufficient to satisfy my needs but I also wanted to get to know the city of Saint-Louis.
>
> (Sadiou/40 years/male/Senegal)

Initially applied only to the migration of young men, the term "faire la jeunesse" also seems increasingly valid for young women. While migration of young men has a long-standing tradition in both study areas, today the migration of young women is considered "à la mode" in both study areas. Most people leave the rural areas at least for a certain time, leaving mainly old people and children in the village. Yaya, a 30-year-old Malian puts it like this:

> We always say, that the village is for the old people. When you are young, you have to go out and to make a living.
>
> (Yaya/30 years/male/Mali)

Differing preferences and aspirations

People have different skills, preferences, ideas, dreams, ambitions, abilities and aspirations. They choose professional activities as well as living and working locations according to their preferences and aspirations, if they have the capability to do so. However, preferences for a location and a profession may be incompatible, for instance, when no corresponding employment is available in the preferred location. Many young people interviewed in the rural areas preferred to migrate or to pursue a professional activity other than agriculture, which requires them to migrate. They highlighted the job opportunities elsewhere, while finding agriculture tiring and ineffective.

Young people – as Aliou (see Box 6.2) – aspire for a better life and no longer consider agriculture as a realistic means to achieve it. A higher living standard or a different lifestyle is difficult to attain without migration because the local market offers few – and often not well-paid – employment opportunities. At the same time, the outcome of agriculture no longer meets young people's demand for consumer goods and their expectations for a certain lifestyle. For many, migration appears to be the easiest, most effective, and probably the only solution to move out of poverty and more generally to succeed in life and to get ahead. As such, migration is often an expression of personal success and progress that goes beyond fulfilling basic needs.

Box 6.2   Aliou

Aliou is a young man from a Senegalese village. Today he is 36 years old and works in Dakar as a businessperson, selling tires. He is the oldest son of his mother. Although he always wanted to, he never went to school because his father wanted him to help on the fields instead. At age 15, Aliou left the village for the first time. The coastal city of Saint-Louis, 3.5 hours away, became his new home for the next two years. During that time, he sold rice in order to support his mother and his family with money. He preferred to leave the village and to try his luck because the revenues from agriculture were uncertain. After two years in Saint-Louis, he returned to the village only to leave four weeks later to join his uncle in Dakar. Through the help of a friend from the village, he quickly found a job in selling tires.

It has been almost 20 years now that Aliou works in Dakar as a businessperson, while his parents, brothers and sisters stay in the village and continue farming. He not only supports the family with the money, but almost all his investments go to the village. He even built a house there because he plans to return to the village once he retires. According to Aliou, Dakar is for working, the village is for the family and living. With respect to agriculture, he explains that *even if there were the perfect conditions for good agriculture, I don't think I would leave my business for agriculture because it gives you no guarantee.* He prefers his work in the city to farming because it is more reliable and more profitable than agriculture. Therefore, he considers the sole reliance on agriculture as irrational and a waste of time and explains why young people want to leave the rural areas.

> That God forgive me for what I am about to say. Our parents in the village wasted their life because of farming. They cultivated during the rainy season and lived from their yields without investing or constructing buildings. This is the reason why those who stayed are today the poorest. And it is also the reason why young people want to leave the village to work.

Not only young men, but also young women often prefer to work in the cities and increasingly leave the rural areas. In contrast to their work in the village, women's work in the cities is usually described as less hard, paid by working hours and acknowledged by others. Korka, a young Malian woman explains the differences in work for women between the cities and the villages in the following excerpt:

> Here in the village, you work but you don't even know what you are doing. You spend the whole day working, but you don't know if it is a waste of time or beneficial. But in the city, you work and you earn something each month.

You also eat well because the food is not the same as in the village. (. . .) The work in the village is more difficult than in Bamako because in the city you work for moments and not like here. Here you work all the time.

(Korka/29 years/female/Mali)

Despite a preference among young interviewees to leave the rural areas and not pursue farming, some young people prefer to continue agriculture and/or to stay in the rural areas. However, not all may have the capability to do. For those who would like to stay but have no interest or are unable to work in agriculture, the local area usually offers limited alternative employment opportunities. Those who prefer to stay in the village emphasise the calmness, cheaper living costs, solidarity of village life and being close to their family as advantages of rural areas. Only a few young people interviewed, such as Modou (see Box 6.3), wanted to stay in the rural areas and continue farming as their main activity. The financial support of his brothers who migrated allows him to pursue his aspirations to stay in the village and work as a farmer.

Box 6.3   Modou

Modou, a 30-year-old farmer, lives in a Senegal village, where he stays all year round in contrast to his brothers and most of his peers. His choice to stay in the village is strongly linked to his wish to be close to his family and to become a successful farmer. Modou is able to stay in the village because in addition to agriculture he works as a guardian, which allows him to complement the revenues from agriculture. Moreover, he can count on his three brothers, working in Dakar and Touba, to provide financial support in years with poor yields.

> I chose to stay because I want to be close to my family. My ambitions are to cultivate and to breed livestock. That's why I stayed in the village. I want to become a great farmer! I never thought about leaving the village or travelling. My brothers didn't want to stay because in the village there is no infrastructure, no water, no electricity. That's why some young people leave to discover other places and to make a living. (. . .) I never left because I am not interested to do so.

In Modou's family – as in most rural households – the household is divided among those who stay and those who migrate. Although livelihood diversification is crucial for most households in the two rural areas, the decision of which household member migrates and which stays is often influenced by people's individual preferences and aspirations. This however presumes that the preconditions to choose between migrating or staying as an option are fulfilled, namely having a sufficient number of male members in working age and different preferences. If not, household members often take turns to migrate. Seydou from Mali illustrates how preferences for moving or staying shape the migration decision within a household:

> In our family, we are five men. We randomly decided who leaves and who stays. If you want to leave, you leave. The big brothers leave and the small ones stay and then they can join us after the rainy season. (. . .) We have one brother who doesn't come to Bamako, he wants to stay in the village. (. . .) Those people, who return for the rainy season, do not have anybody to assist with the cultivation.
>
> (Seydou/45 years/male/Mali)

Education plays a major role in the migration decision and shapes preferences and aspirations. In particular, the highly educated want, and also have to leave the rural areas when they wish to continue their studies, as it is the case for Yacouba (see Box 6.4). Universities are usually only present in the capitals and in very few other big cities in Mali and in Senegal.

Box 6.4   Yacouba

Yacouba came to Bamako in 2008 to pursue his studies at university. As the first-born son of the village chief, Yacouba was obligated by the family to go to a private secondary school in a nearby town. In order to continue his studies at university, which he now aspired to do, he moved to Bamako at the age of 18 where, at that time, the only university in the country was located. This was his first visit to the capital of his country. During the first two months in the city, he stayed at his uncle's, who worked as a guardian. Working with his uncle during his studies allowed him to be more independent. He could afford his own place to stay and finance his education.

Yacouba talks enthusiastically about Bamako's city life:

> I like Bamako very much, it is "formidable" (wonderful).

When asked if he would like to return to the village, he laughs. Returning to the village for good is not an option. He wants to stay in the city. Sometimes he visits his family in the village during harvest, but tries to return to the city as soon as possible. He explains that each time he visits the village, he takes some presents from the city for friends and younger siblings to the village which may in turn fuel their aspirations to migrate to the city:

> I bring some presents for the small children and my friends, like T-shirts, Boubous [traditional clothing for men, author] and other clothes.

Most students like Yacouba usually stay in the city after having completed their studies because they do not find adequate employment in the rural areas. Boys and girls with a secondary education or higher have better employment and vocational prospects elsewhere than in the structurally weak study areas. Continuing small-scale farming as main economic activity is very rare among people with a university degree. Furthermore, strong social obligations deter them from returning to the village. Malik, a student from Senegal, explains how social relationships and social pressure impede his return:

> No, I don't want to return to the village because if I imagine working there as a male nurse in the local health center, people would say: You are the son of. . . . I will not pay because I know your father, he is my friend.
>
> (Malik/20 years/male/Senegal)

This shows that strong social relations and cultural norms impede young educated people from returning to their village due to the fear of not being remunerated for their work. Apart from that, the well-educated feel that returning permanently to "*the rural areas would be a setback*," as expressed by Pape, a student from Dakar. Moreover, the city life usually fascinates young people who can afford to live there. Pape explains the differences between life in the rural areas and the capital that make Dakar so attractive for him.

> If you compare Linguère and Dakar, the difference is obvious: the landscape, the make-up, the way of life. (. . .) I would not use the term "civilised" – that would be too harsh – but there are different comportments between city and village dwellers. Linguère is almost a village in terms of quality of life. People dress differently in Dakar compared to the village people. The climate is different: Dakar is cooler, Linguère is very hot.
>
> (Pape/22 years/male/Senegal)

In Yacouba's village, the first 'son' of the village went to university about 10 years prior to Yacouba's departure. For many remote villages in the rural area, it is still rare to send boys, and even more unusual to send girls to a university. Those who did not have the possibility to go to school or to continue their education usually have different ways to realise their aspirations.

International migration: aspirations for success

International migration to Europe or the USA is often related to aspirations for success. It is mostly perceived as personal and family success going far beyond fulfilling basic needs and supporting the household. International migration from Senegal to Europe has been depicted as a sign of personal success by the interviewees and other studies (c.f. Riccio 2005; Carling et al. 2013). Among the Senegalese interviewees, young men – like Moustapha (see Box 6.5) – aspire for success by migrating to Europe. Success means earning money in order to realise a better life and often a "Western" lifestyle for themselves and their families. Among the Malian interviewees, migration abroad was primarily directed to Abidjan in the Cote d'Ivoire, which seems to be more feasible with respect to risk and cost than migrating outside the continent.

Box 6.5   Moustapha

Moustapha, a 34-year-old man from a Senegalese village characterises a successful international migrant. At first sight, the home of his family differs considerably from other buildings in the village. It is a big white modern house with glass windows and a satellite dish. The European influence is evident. Moustapha's journey began in 1998 with the aim to migrate to Europe. At age 20, he first left the village to Abidjan in the Cote d'Ivoire following rumours that it would be easier to obtain a visa for Europe in the Cote d'Ivoire than in Senegal. Two years later, in June 2000, he entered Italy. With the help of other Senegalese migrants, he found accommodation and started working as an unskilled worker in a factory a month later. These steps were so important to his life that more than 10 years later, he still remembers their exact dates. Moustapha followed his brother to Italy who had migrated in 1993. A few years later, his younger brother joined him in Italy.

Influenced by the success of his older brother, Moustapha's migration to Europe was strongly fuelled by his desire to be successful and to become "somebody". Despite his formal secondary education, Moustapha felt it would be difficult to realise his dreams and aspirations in Senegal because he could earn a greater amount of money in Europe.

> Why Europe? It has been said that there is work and that life is different compared to our lives here. Here in Senegal you work for one or two months and you earn nothing or little. In Europe, in one day, you will be able to earn what you earn here in one or two months. (. . .) The reason I wanted to go to Europe was that in Senegal, there are a lot of people with a degree who don't find a job at all or who don't find an adequate job. I knew it would be difficult to stay here that is why I wanted to do something. (. . .) Even if it would be difficult, what I wanted was to become somebody. I wanted to satisfy the needs of my family and my own needs. (. . .) My goal was to realize something and that was much easier in Europe.

After more than a decade in Europe, he explains that the reality of life in Europe differs from what he had once dreamed. He had and still has to pay a high price for the good life he offers his family. In private he explains that he had suffered a lot during his migration and that he lives under simple and poor conditions in Italy. Moreover, he is seriously affected by the fact that his children are afraid of him because they hardly know him. He is only able to visit the family once a year or even less. Although he would prefer to return to Senegal, this is not an option, because the family demands financial support and is not willing to reduce their luxury standard of living.

Stories of failed migration, awareness campaigns about the risks and costs of migration and discouragement from international migrants may reduce the aspirations of some. Moustapha explains that he strongly discourages other household and village members from migrating to Europe but knows that they will not listen to him just as he did not years earlier. The success stories of earlier migrants, however, still create aspirations for success among many who desire to realise a similar lifestyle.

The current view in literature suggests that international migration is only available for those better off. Nevertheless, the interviews illustrate that international migration can also be a possible means to succeed in life for young people from poor families. Social networks turned out to be more important as a precondition for international migration than financial means. Lacking adequate job opportunities in the country and in the region leaves international migration as the only option to considerably improve the economic status and social standing of migrants and their families. International, interregional or internal migration – whether preferred or not – is often the only option for young people to get ahead and realise their aspirations. International migration, in particular, is related to high costs and risks, and thus represents a desire to succeed in life rather than a response to environmental stressors. Restrictive border controls and visa policies make it difficult to cross international borders and increase the risk and potential suffering of migrants who leave the continent.

Capabilities and aspirations

People do have different capabilities, preferences and aspirations with respect to the decision to migrate or stay (see Figure 3.1). Aliou, Binta, Elhadj, Malik, Modou, Moussa, Moustapha and Yacouba (presented in the Boxes in Chapters 5 and 6) are only some of the people interviewed in the two rural study areas in Mali and in Senegal. They carry different reasons for migrating and staying and have different capabilities to choose freely between the two options. Aliou prefers to work in the city where work is less hard, more profitable and reliable than farming. Moustapha aspires to be successful in Europe and Yacouba wants to continue his studies at university. Malik and Elhadj migrated for adventure and consumer goods at a young age, but returned to the village to start a family. While Malik did not migrate afterwards, Elhadj continued to migrate seasonally to supplement his income from farming with income gained through migration. Although all these people migrated for different reasons, they all had the capability to choose between migrating and staying and preferred to migrate for differing motives. In contrast, Modou chose to stay in the village to become a successful farmer.

Binta and Moussa are less lucky because they cannot choose freely between migrating and staying. Binta, similar to other women from rural Mali, is not allowed to migrate due to restrictions based on patriarchal social norms. Despite prohibition and sanctions of female migration, Binta escaped several times secretly from the village because she wanted to leave. She rebelled against these restrictions, but many women stay because they fear the negative consequences of their action. Moussa, in contrast, would like to stay as a farmer in the rural area, but needs to migrate given his responsibilities to provide for his mother and sister. With no brothers to support him in case of poor yields, he has no other choice than to leave the rural areas and abandon farming as his main economic activity in order to gain his living elsewhere.

If people have the capability to decide between migrating and staying, they usually decide according to their preferences and aspirations. People's capabilities and their preferences and aspirations in the migration decision are crucial for distinguishing if people want or need to stay or to migrate and whether they are "trapped" in an area or forced to leave. This is particularly important for research on the effect of climate change and environmental stressors on migration. The most disadvantaged people are those trapped in staying or forced to leave because they lack the free will to live according to their aspirations and values.

Not all people whose capabilities are restricted to either migrate or stay are necessarily forced to do so. Migrating or staying only becomes forced if people prefer or aspire to an activity that they cannot realise due to a lack of respective capabilities. For instance, some Malian women may prefer to stay in rural areas and thus they may not view their absence of choice to migrate as a problem. They will thus not consider themselves as forced to stay and may not even realise that their capabilities are limited to staying. Farmers who need to leave but prefer to migrate will not necessarily assess their options as limited or consider their migration as a measure of last resort, but rather as an opportunity. Similarly, people who prefer to work outside the agricultural sector often have little choice other than to leave the rural areas, but they may also prefer to leave in order to find better employment. Although this form of migration may not technically be freely made, it is not of a forced character.

It is important that research not only considers people's capabilities to decide whether to migrate or not, but also their preferences and aspirations. This will help to understand why some people stay and others migrate from a certain area despite similar environmental conditions. Moreover, considering people's aspirations and preferences in migration decisions may explain why people move to areas that are also threatened by environmental stress (Black and Bennett et al. 2011). The sole focus on migration as a response to environmental risks cannot explain why people move from one environmentally fragile area to another. This shows that the individual migration motives and aspirations are important determinants of young people's decision to migrate, but they may be hidden behind more socially accepted motives, such as ensuring food security and contributing to the household needs.

What drives migration

Migration from rural areas and the importance of environmental drivers in the region can only be understood when considering the variety of migration reasons and motives. The social-ecological conditions and individual aspirations influence the migration decision in rural areas of the West African Sahel that are affected by environmental degradation and climate change. The main drivers of migration from rural Mali and Senegal include difficult conditions for agriculture, the lack of infrastructure and opportunities in the rural areas, but also perceived opportunities elsewhere, the influence of previous migrants and individual aspirations (see Table 6.1).

Climate change is very likely to worsen the already difficult conditions for agriculture in the rural areas in the future: rising temperatures, increasingly variable rainfalls, decreasing soil fertility and periodical droughts will aggravate the livelihood situation for farmers in the West African Sahel. In addition, poverty and population growth with limited access to fertile land may exacerbate the situation. Lacking financial means impedes investments in seeds, fertiliser, equipment or additional land, which becomes necessary when the soil fertility on the existing fields decreases and population growth at the same time demands higher yields in order to feed the growing number of family members.

The lack of infrastructure and opportunities in the rural areas is another important driver of migration. Rural areas often lack industries and services – and thus opportunities for employment either as a complementary or as an alternative activity to agriculture – and adequate health or schooling infrastructure, particularly for higher education. This makes life in the rural areas not only harder and less attractive for people but also encourages them to leave the areas in search of (better) education, vocation and employment.

The influence of previous migration experiences of other household or community members has a considerable impact on people's migration decision and makes migration of other members more likely. It creates social networks that facilitate the migration of other members. Moreover, migration usually increases the economic situation of the migrant and her/his household, which creates inequalities within and between households and in turn may increase social expectations for migration, but also aspirations to migrate. This process leads to social changes in the home community, such as higher living standards, changes in attitudes and appearance or changes in traditional norms. It can also create a "culture of migration" (Massey et al. 1993) in a community or society, which makes it difficult to act against expectations for migration. Previous migration experiences also spark individual aspirations to achieve the same (or a higher) lifestyle as others.

Table 6.1 Drivers of migration in the study areas.

	Drivers of migration	Detailed aspects

Social-ecological conditions of migration	Difficult conditions for small-scale agriculture	• Seasonality – no work in agriculture during the dry season
		• Low and uncertain yields due to negative climate and environmental changes, such as:
		  • Increasingly variable rainfall and overall reduction in net precipitation during the rainy season
		  • Decreasing soil fertility
		  • Crop pests (mainly Senegal)
		  • Extreme events such as droughts (and floods in Mali)
		• Lack of financial means to invest in agriculture (in seeds, fertiliser and material)
		• Lack of fertile land due to population growth (only Mali)

	Lack of infrastructure and opportunities	• Lack of industries and services in the communities and the regions => no employment opportunities outside the agricultural sector • Lack of accessible schools (particularly secondary education) and universities • Better opportunities for education, vocation and employment elsewhere
	Influence of previous migrations	• Social networks facilitate subsequent migration • Social inequality in social standing and economic situation in the family or community increases • Positive assessment of migration and perpetuation of migration • Social expectation related to migration • Trends and peer pressure among young men and women • Social change towards a "modern" lifestyle
Individual aspirations and preferences	Increased aspirations – particularly among young people	• Increasing aspirations for higher living standards and consumer goods • Aspirations for economic independence, a better economic situation and social standing • Increasing desire for consumer goods and a preference for a "modern" lifestyle • Achieve greater autonomy and escape narrow traditional social norms, demarcation from parents and rural life • Discover the world outside the village, gain experience and skills • Unwillingness to work in agriculture • Ambitions to succeed in life and to "get ahead"

Source: Author.

Individual aspiration, particularly among young people, often includes their desire for a better future, economic independence and consumer goods, greater autonomy from the parents and the traditional social norms in the villages, e.g. postponing or avoiding arranged marriage. This is often related to a demarcation from rural people and rural lifestyle and the unwillingness to continue the hard work in agriculture with little revenues, often combined with ambitions for personal success. Non-economic aspirations, such as curiosity and the desire to discover the world outside the village and at the same time gaining life experiences and different skills not available in the rural areas, further stimulate people's aspirations.

The different main drivers of migration also shape people's capabilities to migrate or to stay in different ways. In general, the level of voluntariness for migration increases from structural drivers of migration to more individual migration motives. Difficult conditions for small-scale agriculture, for instance, are the most likely to create a necessity to migrate for survival reasons, while migration driven by individual aspirations expresses a desire rather than a need. How social changes can shape people's motives and capabilities to migrate is highlighted in the next chapter.

Bibliography

Black, R., Bennett, S.R.G., Thomas, S.M. and Beddington, J.R. 2011 "Migration as adaptation" *Nature*, 478, 447–449.

Carling, J., Fall, P.D., Hernández-Carretero, M., Sarr, M.Y. and Wu, J. 2013 *Migration aspirations in Senegal: Who wants to leave and why does it matter?* (European Policy Brief), Brussels: European Commission.

de Bruijn, M. and van Dijk, H. 2004 "The importance of socio-cultural differences and of pathway analysis for understanding local actors' responses", in Dietz, A.J., Ruben, R. and Verhagen, A. eds. *The impact of climate change on drylands: With a focus on West Africa* (Environment & Policy, 39), Dordrecht, The Netherlands: Springer Science + Business Media Inc, 341–362.

Graw, K. and Schielke, J.S. 2012 "Introduction: reflections on migratory expectations in Africa and beyond", in Schielke, J.S. and Graw, K. eds. *The global horizon: Expectations of migration in Africa and the Middle East*, Leuven: Leuven University Press, 7–22.

IRIN News 2006 "Mankind is like this: One want to get ahead", October 31. Senegal, Dakar. www.irinnews.org/report/61454/senegal-mankind-is-like-this-one-wants-to-get-ahead

Massey, D.S., Arango, J., Hugo, G., Kouaouci, A., Pellegrino, A. and Taylor, J.E. 1993 "Theories of international migration: a review and appraisal" *Population and Development Review*, 19(3), 431–466.

Riccio, B. 2005 "Talkin' about migration – some ethnographic notes on the ambivalent representation of migrants in contemporary Senegal" *Wiener Zeitschrift für kritische Afrikastudien*, 5(8), 99–118.

Schapendonk, J. 2010 "Staying put in moving sands: The stepwise migration process of sub-Saharan African Migrants heading North", in Engel, U. and Nugent, P. eds. *Respacing Africa* (African-Europe Group for Interdisciplinary Studies, 4), Leiden: Brill, 113–138.

7   Social transformation and its impact on the effects of climate change

Social change, social transformation and migration

Social change and social transformation are terms for designating changes in societies. Although they have slightly different meanings, they are often used synonymously. Social change can imply changes in a single sector of a society, while social transformation describes more profound changes in a society, such as the industrial revolution and colonialism, but also long-term economic development. Social change is present in all societies and can arise from different factors including contact with other societies (diffusion), changes in environmental conditions, technological evolutions, political movements, economic developments, demographical changes or ideologies (Gillin and Gillin 1942). Social transformation is "a fundamental shift in the way society is organised that goes beyond the continual processes of incremental social change that are always at work" (Castles 2010: 1576).

Mobility has always contributed to changes in cultures (Massey 1998; Castles 2010; Hahn 2013) and can be both a consequence or a cause of social change, as well as more profound social transformation. Migration can lead to transformation in both sending and receiving areas; however change is more likely to occur in societies of origin (Portes 2010). The migrants' economic remittances can initiate, but also respond to social changes and transformation in the home country, region and community (Portes 2010; Aksakal et al. 2016). Remittances are usually spent on food, healthcare, housing and education of other household members and can thus contribute to changes in different areas of life. Moreover, social remittances can transform social and political life in the sending communities or countries (Levitt 1998). Migrants transfer ideas, behaviours, identities and social capital when they return to their communities of origin or communicate with household members or friends from these areas. Their experiences lead to an exchange of practices and a transfer of skills and knowledge to the sending areas. They also influence people's opinions and attitudes and therewith can change social norms by reinforcing traditional norms or by establishing new ones (de Haan 2000; Van Hear 2010).

Changes initiated by migration in people's home community influence the migration behaviour of other community members. Forms of social change in developing countries that can cause migration are, among others, the destruction of rural livelihoods, changes in the environment or erosion of local social orders (Castles 2009). Environmental and social processes are often interlinked. Environmental change, for instance, can cause migration and social change, but may also be a result of both processes. On the one hand, unfavourable environmental conditions may foster rural-urban migration contributing to increasing urbanisation and the declining importance of the agricultural sector and rural livelihood. Consequently, this may lead to further social change in the sending and receiving areas. On the other hand, social change or transformation, such as urbanisation and industrialisation may cause negative environmental effects, such as air pollution, increasing temperatures or other climate changes, but may also cause positive change in the environment. For example, the soil may recover due to a lower population density and less pressure on the land contributing to less intensive land use.

Contemporary change processes, such as urbanisation or economic development, are often based on migration processes, not only in West Africa but also globally. Nevertheless, there is a tendency in research to see migration as distinct from broader social relationships and change processes instead of understanding migration as a part of society and its social transformations (Castles 2010). The strong relationship between migration and social changes raises questions about how mobility affects change in any society, and not – as this is often the case for research on migration in Africa – to discuss migration only as an exceptional problem for the poor (Bakewell 2008).

In the West African Sahel, climate change may have far reaching consequences in the region. At the same time, social changes are likely to affect people's dependency on agriculture, therefore increase or reduce the potential impact of climate change on people's livelihood and migration. In rural Mali and Senegal, a high population growth may, for instance, worsen the livelihood situation of the rural population and endanger their food security. In contrast, an increasing level of education and aspirations among young people for a different life may contribute to less dependency on agriculture and decrease the impact of climate change on people's livelihoods and migration. Migration in the West African Sahel has contributed to substantial social changes in the past and will continue to propel social transformation processes now and in the future. Social change in many sectors of societies, such as increasing literacy, population growth and urbanisation, may transform rural communities and life in West African societies and influence the impact of climate change on people's livelihoods and migration.

Success stories of migration and social change

Migration from environmentally fragile areas is not necessarily a result of worsening environmental and socio-economic conditions, but may be linked to better opportunities elsewhere. It is often encouraged by the migration of other household or community members who have previously left. Migration begins for a variety of reasons, but the reasons that initiated migration may be different from those that perpetuate it. In the West African Sahel, the droughts during the

1970s and 1980s initiated, or at least intensified, people's mobility. In the beginning, migration was assumed to be a reaction to difficult living conditions caused by severe droughts and financial crisis. Later, migration, particularly international migration, became a model for social rise as a result of the success stories of earlier emigrants (Fall 2003; Gerdes 2007; Bleibaum 2009). The remittances and goods that migrants sent and brought back home led to development and improved livelihoods. It also changed the social status of the migrant and his household. In general, causation becomes cumulative by migration altering the social context within which subsequent migration decisions are made (Massey et al. 1993). Migration typically makes migration more likely and in that way it sustains itself.

In addition to the economic impact, the success of previous migrants often creates a positive image of the migrant that others aim to imitate. This leads to a *culture of migration* (Massey et al. 1993: 452). The *culture of migration* refers to a development in which migration contributes to a stronger desire for consumer goods and social standing within a community. People often wish to copy the migrant success story and want to realise the same diet, lifestyle, leisure activities and amenities as one's neighbour, reference group, or society. Along with the desire for social prestige, the success of the migrants influences the individual aspirations of others and their motivation to migrate decisively (Stark and Taylor 1989; Massey 1998; Doevenspeck 2011). Eventually migration becomes a socially respected and expected aspect of the community which changes its social norms and values (Massey et al. 1993; Stark 2003).

Figure 7.1 illustrates how migration sustains itself. Migrants send remittances back home and return to the village with goods that are not known or not available in rural areas. The migration of one or several household members usually improves the household's income and contributes to a general development of the community. However, the economic improvement of a household also creates or increases economic inequalities and social differentiation within and between households and rural communities (Francis and Hoddinott 1993; Massey et al. 1993; Ellis 1998; de Haan 1999; Tacoli 2011). In turn, it heightens people's desire to improve their income relative to other households or to their reference groups and to be able to realise the same lifestyle as migrants (Stark and Taylor 1989; Massey et al. 1993; Czaika and de Haas 2011). Economic and human development increase people's capabilities and aspirations to achieve the same or higher lifestyle than others (de Haas 2010), but also creates social expectations on young men to contribute to the household income. The migrant's remittances, their changed appearance, experiences and ideas lead to development and can change norms and tastes in the community, when people try to adopt this style. Realising one's aspirations and a different lifestyle demands more cash and goods. Labour migration is often the only effective way for people in rural areas to achieve these goals. At the same time, social networks, built by previous migrants, facilitate the migration for others. This makes it more likely that people choose to migrate.

In the two rural areas in Mali and Senegal, the success of earlier migrants has changed the appearance of many villages and its residents in different ways. People portray impressively how the success of the migrants has changed the community.

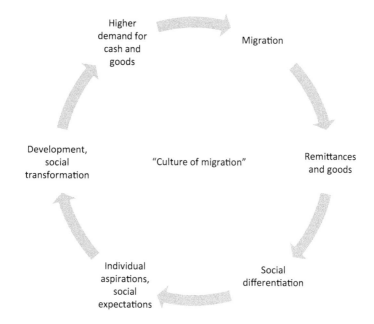

Figure 7.1 Migration as cause and consequence of development.
Source: Author.

The first migrants brought European clothing, bicycles and other goods to the village: "extraordinary" things they had never seen before. Migrant households' were the first to afford electricity, modern toilets and houses constructed with modern materials that replaced straw huts. But the migrants' money not only benefited the migrant and his household, but contributed to the development of the village by financing infrastructure, such as schools and health centres. The cash from earlier migrants moreover corresponded to the increasing demand for financial means, a consequence of increasing monetisation and development. Aliou, a man from Senegal, shares his souvenirs about the developments in the village and the role of migration in these changes:

> In my village, there was no electricity; the houses were made of straw with barbed wire. But that has changed. Those who left returned and constructed houses of hard materials. They installed electricity and built modern toilets. (. . .) You know, we have been cultivating for a long time, but nothing has ever changed. If it wasn't for migration, all these changes would not have happened. Well, I could observe this, even though I am still young, all these changes happened not at a time when everybody cultivated, but at the time when the young started to leave to work elsewhere.
>
> (Aliou/36 years/male/Senegal)

Today, households with international migrant members are often particularly wealthy compared to other households in the community. This is obvious when entering a village. Successful migration allows a lifestyle for the migrant and the household that a "simple farmer" would not be able to afford and often results in social upward mobility.

In the two rural areas of Bandiagara and Linguère, the success of migrants and the income differential within and between households had, and still has, a considerable impact on people's decision to migrate. Young people often wish to copy the migrant success story, want to offer their family a similar or even higher living standard and want to be able to live a similar lifestyle as others. The change, in terms of style (e.g. clothing, jewellery etc.) and consumer goods, within a household and a community, creates aspirations in other members to afford a similar life. Some young people are more open to the influence of the migrants because they want to be more like those in the "rich" and "modern" receiving community (Levitt 1998). For them, migration often seems to be the only feasible way to realise these aspirations.

> When a person leaves and returns with lots of goods, such as radios, mobile phones, etc., other people want to do the same things, they want to imitate them.
>
> (Baba Yatta/70 years/male/Senegal)

The economic success of earlier migrants and their contributions to the economic well-being of the household and the community also changed people's attitudes towards migration. When people realised that migration could offer a better future for young people from the villages, it became more and more accepted as illustrated in the following quote by a Senegalese man:

> In earlier times, the people in the village were hostile to the idea of people leaving to work elsewhere. With the success of those who left for work, the mentality started to change and the elderly understood that leaving could offer real perspectives of success for young people from the village.
>
> (Aliou/36 years/male/Senegal)

Today, in the two rural study areas there is a positive image of the migrant and migration of young men is not only widely accepted but also even expected. An increase in migration is thus not necessarily a result of worsening environmental and socio-economic conditions, but might be linked to economic incentives or (the expectation of) better opportunities elsewhere and individual aspirations to a different lifestyle encouraged by previous migrations and social networks.

Population growth and urbanisation

A high population growth in both countries is very likely to imperil the livelihoods of the rural population and increase the need to migrate in order to ensure the household's food security. Population growth is high in Mali and in Senegal at an average rate of 3% (UN Population Division 2015). In remote rural areas, however, population growth is often even higher due to a lower level of education and limited access and/or cultural reservation against birth control measures. A Malian woman gives birth to five children on average. As in most African societies, the majority of the population in Mali and Senegal is very young. Almost half of Mali's population is under 15 years of age and 67% of the population is under 24. In Senegal, the percentage of people under 15 has slightly decreased from 48% in 1986 to 44% in 2015, but still 63% of the population is under 24 (UN Population Division 2015).

The high population growth, in combination with a limited access to fertile land, may worsen the livelihood situation of the people in the Sahel and increase their need to leave the rural area in the future. A high population growth increases the pressure on the land and natural resources because already scarce areas of fertile, cultivable land have to be shared among more people as well as provide food for an increasing number of people. This leads to overexploitation of the land which results not only in lower yields but also in increasing land degradation. While the Senegalese indicate that the availability of land is not yet a problem, it seems to be a major issue in the rocky soils of the Dogon plateau in Mali. In addition, the political crisis in Mali and the loss of tourism as a source of income certainly has increased pressure to migrate from the Dogon country in order to cope with current and future risks (see Box 7.1). Conflicts related to natural resources and land, mainly between crop farmers and livestock breeders, have increased and are likely to do so in the future. In Mali the easy access to fire weapons due to the crisis in the North of the country makes conflicts over land and resources increasingly violent.

Box 7.1   Political crisis in Mali

The political crisis in Mali, which led to a military coup in March 2012 and an armed conflict in the North of the country, has had effects on people's livelihood in the research area but probably also on other parts of the country. The Malian study area chosen for this book is also known as the Dogon country, named after the main ethnicity living in the area. The Dogon country used to be an attractive tourist destination for individual travellers during the 1990s and the first decade of the millennium. Tourism was an important source of income for the rural population in the region on top of their traditional crop farming activities. Increasing activity of the terrorist group Al-Qaida Maghreb in the Northern Sahara, particularly the threat of kidnapping Westerners, had already reduced the number of tourists visiting the Dogon country in the years prior to the military coup. Tourism, however, totally collapsed with the military coup in 2012. People from the Dogon land, which borders the Northern parts of the country, all of a sudden lost tourism as one of their main local income sources. Crop farming alone does not allow a similar standard of living and makes farmers more vulnerable to environmental stress and other external risks, in particular food security. Although the research for this book took place just before the military coup, it seems quite likely that the crisis and the loss of tourism increased people's need to migrate from the Dogon country.

The crisis and the loss of tourism has additionally impeded or at least decelerated development and social changes previously initiated by tourism. Interviewees indicated that tourists brought Western values and culture to the Dogon country. Yacouba, a young man from such a village, states that "*the European life came little by little to the village*," and contributed to various social changes in the respective villages. Tourists financed schools and teachers under the condition that both boys and girls attend formal schooling that consequently led to greater education of girls and changing perceptions of gender roles.

A high vulnerability to external stressors and poverty also increases the risk of being influenced by religious extremists and terrorist groups, active in the north of Mali. In particular, young men from rural areas with a low level of education and little opportunities for their future may become an easy target for terrorist groups. While literacy rates have risen in both countries, schools in Northern Mali have been closed for months and even for years since the start of the conflict, depriving a whole generation of young people from opportunities for their future. Increasing radicalisation among young people could become a further destabilisation factor for the country and the whole region, potentially triggering more migration and flight within the region and to Europe.

Population growth is likely to increase the pressure to migrate while environmental degradation and climate change may aggravate the situation and increase the number of environmental migrants. Nevertheless, the rural exodus of young people is not only caused by a need to leave the rural areas, but also by an increasing desire of young people to retreat from agriculture.

Urban living will be the dominant lifestyle in the future, not only in the "global North" but also in the "global South". Over half of the world's population lives in urban areas today and millions of people migrate to cities each year. Urban areas and their population are also rapidly increasing in both Mali and Senegal. Today 40% of Malians live in cities compared to only 28% in the year 2000. In Senegal, 44% of the population live in urban areas compared to 40% in 2000 (UN Population Division 2015). Approximately one-third of the urban population in Mali and Senegal lives in the capitals of Bamako and Dakar. Future urbanisation will continue to increase in both countries with an urban growth rate for Senegal at 3.6% and for Mali at 5%. By 2030, more than half of the Malian and Senegalese population will live in urban areas. While the urban population grows rapidly, the required infrastructure and the formal employment opportunities are not developing at the same rate. The consequences are often poverty, difficult living conditions and high levels of unemployment in the cities. Nevertheless, rural-urban migration continues. It often results from the erosion of older forms of rural production and the growth of new urban opportunities (Castles 2012). A general shift in society from agricultural activities to non-agricultural activities and from food production to food purchase is likely to reduce people's dependency on agriculture and their vulnerability to environmental stress. It may, however, increase the dependency of the rural population on remittances and therefore exacerbate the pressure on migrants to financially support the household.

Young people's retreat from agriculture

Rural-urban migration could be partly a means to adapt to, or to cope with unfavourable social-ecological conditions in the sending areas, but could also be a result of increasing development, education and individual aspirations to an urban lifestyle. Recent literature suggests that young people in the Sahel increasingly leave the rural areas and the agricultural sector. Mertz et al. found in their study on climate and adaptation in West Africa that people's main sources of income – rain-fed crops and livestock – had decreased over the past 20 years, while income, which in general is heavily migration-based, has increased. Moreover, people in the driest zone of their study areas had a "resigned attitude toward crop production" (Mertz et al. 2010: 8). A study on climate change and migration in Malawi indicates that for young Malawians, villages are "boring and difficult places to live" (Suckall et al. 2016: 11). The interviewees express that farming is becoming harder and that migration aspirations of young people are becoming stronger, partly "due to a desire to leave behind a life based on agriculture and experience a life of freedom and excitement in town" (Suckall et al. 2016: 11). Nevertheless, the study finds that the majority of the people still want to stay in the rural areas. The authors, however, note that their findings may only be applicable in countries where urbanisation is relatively recent (Suckall et al. 2016). In Malawi only 16% of the population lives in urban areas; thus, urbanisation is much lower than in West African countries.

Other studies on climate change and migration in Mexico and Ethiopia find that young people in rural areas often perceive farming as hard work that does not offer enough stable revenues because it is highly dependent on unreliable weather conditions (Schmidt-Verkerk 2011; Morrissey 2012). Moreover, young people consider rural life in general undesirable because it is hard and monotonous (i.e. same food every day and old clothes) (Morrissey 2012), making it less appealing for them. Rather than working in agriculture, young people often imagine their future without poverty through the opportunities offered by migration (van der Geest 2009; Schmidt-Verkerk 2011; Morrissey 2012). A change to "urban" tastes and changes in lifestyles often breaks with the traditions of parents and, due to their higher costs, are usually difficult to attain through local labour (Massey et al. 1993; de Haas 2010; Schmidt-Verkerk 2011). This generates aspirations among young people to leave the rural areas and the agricultural sector. The increasing rural exodus is also encouraged by parents. A study on identity, environment and development in Guinea-Bissau, for instance, shows that parents often wish for their children to go to school and leave rural areas in order to have a better life. One interviewee in Davidson's study on Guinea-Bissau states, "that's the only thing we wish for the future of our children: that they don't stay here" (Davidson 2016: 174).

Young people in Mali and Senegal increasingly desire to leave the agricultural sector, but do not find alternative local employment in the rural areas. The lack of local employment opportunities has been referred to as "the biggest challenge faced by the populations who are no less committed to their land" (Fall et al. 2010: 39). Caused by a weak regional economy and poor infrastructure, it is the main reason for the rural exodus in Senegal (ANSD 2010). Moreover, improved means of transportation and communication to stay in touch with family back home facilitate migration to urban centres. Young men from the two rural areas around Bandiagara and Linguère also explain that they want to leave the agricultural sector and are increasingly doing so. Many of them prefer to migrate to the cities in order to find long-term employment. Migration from both rural areas is no longer just a seasonal supplemental activity to agriculture, but becomes a temporary or long-term activity for many people.

A group of young men in Mali explain that once they have found a relatively well-paid job during the course of their migration, they often prefer to stay in migration due to a fixed contract and more reliable income than to return for the harvest:

> If you find a good job over there, where you earn well, you prefer to buy [food, author] and send it because if you quit your job in order to return to the village, someone else will take the job and you cannot get it back when you return. That is why this people prefer to stay and to send what they earn to the village.
>
> (Group of young men/Mali)

Although many people from the areas do have a strong attachment to the land and rural areas, they prefer to work in the cities where work is usually more profitable and reliable than agriculture. In contrast, they consider farming hard work and the revenues highly unreliable due to the unstable environmental conditions. The case of Aliou (see Box 6.2) is a good example of young people from both study areas who are looking for a better life in the cities and do not want to continue the work on the fields for several reasons.

The survey findings suggest that in addition to the qualitative interviews, the retreat from agriculture and from rural areas is a growing phenomenon in Mali and Senegal. The youngest survey participants, aged 18 to 30 years old, are less likely to depend on agriculture (36%) compared to the 31 to 50 year olds (52%) and those 50 years or older (62%). The percentage of the youngest group involved in agriculture was lower in Senegal than in Mali (30% versus 41%). The youngest also had different migration motives than older respondents.

Young people were less likely to state environmental reasons for their migrations and instead, migrated for individual motives, such as education or vocational training, clothes, adventure or visits. Indeed, young migrants have always
ranked other migration motives above "food security" because the responsibility
for the household is lower at a younger age. Nevertheless, migration motives
differ among young migrants depending on the time of migration. Environmental reasons have been less important for young people's migration in recent years
(2000–12) compared to the migration of young people in earlier decades (19%
compared to 33% in the 1970s, 45% in the 1980s and 35% in the 1990s).

The increasing reluctance among young people to pursue agriculture and/or
a rural life is not only the result of increasingly difficult environmental conditions, population growth and the relatively low revenues gained from agriculture.
The difficult conditions may accelerate the rural exodus, but cultural and social
change, such as a culture of migration, lifestyle changes, higher levels of education and individual aspirations for a better or different life, are also important
drivers of migration from both rural areas. Migration, whether it is preferred or
not, is often the only option for people to get ahead and to realise their personal
needs and aspirations. The increasing retreat of young people from agriculture
makes them less dependent on the natural environment, therefore reducing
the impact of climate change and environmental stressors on the livelihoods of
migrants and their families.

Educating to counter environmental stress

Formal education as a factor of social change matters with respect to the impact
of climate change on livelihoods and migration in rural areas. People with a
secondary level of education or higher have better employment opportunities
and are less likely to work as farmers. Consequently, environmental stress is less
likely to affect their livelihoods. In Mali and Senegal, the level of education has
increased considerably over the last decades, particularly among young people.
The literacy rate among 15- to 24-year-old youths increased in Senegal from 49%
in the year 2000 to 65% in 2010 and an estimated 73% in 2015. In Mali, the
youth literacy rate was much lower, but increased from 27% in 2000 to 44% in
2010 and an estimated 53% in 2015 (UNESCO-UIS 2012). Public education in
Mali and Senegal is, in principle, provided free of charge and is compulsory for
nine years. In reality, however, many children, particularly in rural areas, do not
attend school. The net primary school enrolment in the district of Louga in Senegal is 45% compared to 58% as the national average and is equally distributed
between boys and girls (ANSD 2014). The enrolment of boys and girls at the
primary school level in the district of Mopti in Mali is at 35%, the lowest in the
country, compared to the national average of 54% (INSTAT 2014b). Literacy
rate is often below the national average in rural areas, but policy programmes
have still resulted in an improvement of school enrolment in remote areas.

The increase in formal education is also noticeable in both rural study areas.
The level of formal education was highest among the youngest survey participants, the 18 to 30 year olds. In this group, 21% indicated at least a secondary

education, compared to 7% in the middle age group (31 to 50yearsold) and 3% among 50 year olds or higher. However, even among the youngest group, the level of education is still low, with 61% of the 18 to 30 year olds not having received formal schooling. The share of young people without formal schooling differs strongly between the two areas with 52% of Senegalese having no formal education compared to 70% in Mali. With respect to gender, the level of education is generally lower among the female respondents as compared to male participants in both countries (van der Land and Hummel 2013).

The school enrolment and the higher education of girls have increased, even though boys still dominate the classes, particularly in rural areas. A Senegalese student explains, for instance, that the number of boys represented three-quarters of his class in secondary school. The larger number of boys in school results mainly from the tradition of not sending girls to school or only to primary school in rural areas. Many villagers still prefer that their daughters marry at a young age instead of sending them to school. Moreover, reservations against the education of girls also exist with respect for higher education. Households, mainly the head of the households, often think that girls should not continue their studies after secondary education either because they are not able to pay their studies or prefer them to marry. They also fear that the girls may change their behaviour in the city far from their control and authority and not respect traditional norms anymore. The liberty experienced as a student in the city often changes young people's attitudes, opinions and the way they dress.

In general, the level of education has improved for both boys and girls in the rural areas due to programmes by the government and international organisations that foster education and as a result of awareness campaigns on the importance of education for the future of children. In addition to policy and development programmes, the remittances of migrants also contribute to improving the level of education. Interviewees from both areas explain that the remittances of migrants help finance the construction of schools and to pay teachers.

People with a formal education higher than primary level were less likely to work as farmers and thus, were less vulnerable to environmental stress than people with no or a low level of formal education. Although the level of education did not influence the propensity to migrate among the survey participants, the better educated migrated for reasons other than the environment. Agriculture is a main economic activity for 58% of the survey participants with no formal education, but only for 18% of participants with a high level of education (secondary level and higher). While the survey only included very few people at a university level, national survey data for Mali shows that the number is even lower for people with a university degree: only 6% of people with a university education work in agriculture compared to 73% of people with no education (INSTAT 2014a). People with a higher education, who stayed or returned to the study areas, were mainly involved in business or in other sectors, such as administration, health or teaching – activities that are not directly dependent on climatic or environmental factors.

Girls and boys with a secondary education or higher have usually far better employment and vocational prospects in the urban centres than in the structurally weak rural areas. Therefore, it is not surprising that the better educated more often migrate for education or vocational reasons than for economic or environmental reasons. Some 55% of the educated migrate for better learning and/or vocational training opportunities; this applies only to 9% of participants with a primary education and to 6% with no formal education. People with no formal education or only primary education (69% and 70%) primarily migrate for economic reasons, while the well-educated expressed far less agreement to this motive (26%). Only 5% of people with a secondary education migrated due to environmental reasons compared to 19% of those with a lower formal education. Therefore, it is rather unlikely that the well-educated migrate in response to environmental stress and unfavourable conditions. In contrast, it seems that with an increasing level of education, young people will more likely leave the rural areas for longer periods and not continue to work in (small-scale) agriculture. Or to put it in the words of an elderly man from Senegal: *The 'stupid' ones and those who did not succeed in school stay in the village, while the smart people leave.*

The literacy rate and the level of education have risen in absolute and relative numbers so far and are likely to do so in the future. With a growing level of education, people become less dependent on agriculture and less vulnerable to future climate change. The changes to higher education in both countries may mitigate the impact of climate change and environmental stress on people's livelihoods and thus "environmental migration".

Social changes may lead to a broader social transformation in the West African Sahel and may either aggravate or reduce the effects of climate change and environmental stress on people's livelihoods and mobility. Negative climate changes, like rising temperatures and an increasing variability of rainfall, may considerably worsen the food security situation in the West African Sahel. The effects of climate change can have particularly deteriorating effects on people's livelihoods when other structural factors already put people's livelihoods at risk. Social changes, such as a high population growth, the loss of an important source of income and/or political crises, can create conditions whereby climate change can accelerate the deterioration. As a consequence, the need to migrate from the rural areas may increase and augment the number of "environmental migrants". At the same time, social changes, like increasing development, education and urbanisation, are likely to decrease people's dependency on agriculture and therefore reduce their vulnerability to environmental stress. Social change and transformation processes may thus mitigate the impact of climate change on people's livelihoods and release the pressure to migrate due to environmental stress in the West African Sahel, despite worsening climate conditions.

Bibliography

Aksakal, M., Schmidt, K. and Faist, T. 2016 *Social transformation and migration: Unveiling the nexus* (COMCAD Working Papers 147), Bielefeld: Center on Migration, Citizenship and Development.

ANSD 2010 *Situation économique et sociale de la région de Louga 2010* (Service Régional de la Statistique et de la Démographie: Louga), Agence Nationale de la Statistique et de la Démographie (ANSD).

ANSD 2014 *Rapport definitif RGPHAE 2013. Recensement Général de la Population et de l'Habitat, de l'Agriculture et de l'Elevage*, Agence Nationale de la Statistique et de la Démographie (ANSD).

Bakewell, O. 2008 "'Keeping them in their place': The ambivalent relationship between development and migration in Africa" *Third World Quarterly*, 29(7), 1341–1358.

Bleibaum, F. 2009 *Environmental change and forced migration scenarios*, Senegal: Case Study Report (EACH-FOR) Project.

Castles, S. 2009 "Development and migration – migration and development: What comes first? Global perspective and African experiences" *Theoria*, 56(121), 1–31.

Castles, S. 2010 "Understanding global migration: A social transformation perspective" *Journal of Ethnic and Migration Studies*, 36(10), 1565–1586.

Castles, S. 2012 "Understanding the relationship between methodology and methods", in Vargas-Silva, C. ed. *Handbook of research methods in migration*, Cheltenham: Edward Elgar, 7–25.

Czaika, M. and de Haas, H. 2011 *The role of internal and international relative deprivation in global migration. DEMIG project paper no. 5* (Working Papers 35), Oxford: International Migration Institute (IMI), University of Oxford.

Davidson, J. 2016 *Sacred rice: an ethnography of identity, environment, and development in rural West Africa* (Issues of globalization), New York: Oxford University Press.

de Haan, A. 1999 "Livelihoods and poverty: the role of migration - a critical review of the migration literature" *Journal of Development Studies*, 36(2), 1–47.

de Haan, A. 2000 *Migrants, livelihoods and rights: The relevance of migration in development policies*, Social Development Working Paper.

de Haas, H. 2010 "Migration and development: A theoretical perspective" *International Migration Review*, 44(1), 227–264.

Doevenspeck, M. 2011 "The thin line between choice and flight: Environment and migration in rural Benin" *International Migration*, 49, e50–e68.

Ellis, F. 1998 "Household strategies and rural livelihood diversification" *The Journal of Development Studies*, 35(1), 1–38.

Fall, A.S. 2003 *Enjeux et défis de la migration internationale de travail ouest-africaine* (Cahiers de migrations internationales 62F), Geneva: International Labour Office.

Fall, P.D., Hernández, M.C. and Sarr, M.Y. 2010 *Senegal. Country and research areas report* (Eumagine - Project Paper 2), Université Cheikh Anta Diop de Dakar (UCAD); Peace Research Institute Oslo (PRIO).

Francis, E. and Hoddinott, J. 1993 "Migration and differentiation in Western Kenya: A tale of two sub-locations" *The Journal of Development Studies*, 30(1), 115–145.

Gerdes, F. 2007 *Länderprofil Senegal* (focus Migration 10), Bundeszentrale für politische Bildung und Hamburgisches WeltWirtschaftsInstitut.

Gillin, J.L. and Gillin, J.P. 1942 *An introduction to sociology*, New York: Macmillan.

Hahn, H.P. 2013 "Immer im Aufbruch: Die Menschheit unterwegs: Formen der Mobilität und soziale Identität" *Das Wissenschaftsmagazin Forschung Frankfurt: Thema Mobilität*, 31(2), 22–26.

INSTAT 2014a *Accessibilité aux soins de santé, mobilité, vie politique et associative et dépenses de consommation des ménages.* Rapport d'analyse deuxième passage: juillet – septembre 2013 (Enquête modulaire et permanente auprès des ménages (EMOP)), Bamako, Mali: Institut National de la Statistique du Mali.

INSTAT 2014b *Enquête modulaire et permanente auprès des ménages (EMOP).* Rapport d'analyse premier passage 2014, Bamako, Mali: Institut National de la Statistique du Mali.

Levitt, P. 1998 "Social remittances: migration driven local-level forms of cultural diffusion" *International Migration Review*, 32(4), 926–948.

Massey, D.S. 1998 *Worlds in motion: Understanding international migration at the end of the millennium* (International studies in demography), Oxford, New York: Clarendon Press; Oxford University Press.

Massey, D.S., Arango, J., Hugo, G., Kouaouci, A., Pellegrino, A. and Taylor, J.E. 1993 "Theories of international migration: a review and appraisal" *Population and Development Review*, 19(3), 431–466.

Mertz, O., Mbow, C., Østergaard Nielsen, J., Maiga, A., Diallo, D., Reenberg, A., Diouf, A., Barbier, B., Moussa, I.B., Zorom, M., Ouattara, I. and Dabi, D. 2010 "Climate factors play a limited role for past adaptation strategies in West Africa" *Ecology and Society*, 15(4), 25.

Morrissey, J. 2012 "Contextualizing links between migration and environmental change in northern Ethiopia", in Hastrup, K. and Fog Olwig, K. eds. *Climate change and human mobility: global challenges to the social sciences*, Cambridge: Cambridge University Press, 110–146.

Portes, A. 2010 "Migration and social change: Some conceptual reflections" *Journal of Ethnic and Migration Studies*, 36(10), 1537–1563.

Schmidt-Verkerk, K. 2011 *The potential influence of climate change on migratory behaviour – a study of drought, hurricanes and migration in Mexico*. Dissertation. University of Sussex.

Stark, O. 2003 *Tales of migration without wage differentials: Individual, family and community contexts* (ZEF Discussion Papers on Development Policy 73), Bonn: Zentrum für Entwicklungsforschung.

Stark, O. and Taylor, J.E. 1989 "Relative deprivation and international migration" *Demography*, 26(1), 1–14.

Suckall, N., Fraser, E. and Forster, P. 2016 "Reduced migration under climate change: Evidence from Malawi using an aspirations and capabilities framework" *Climate and Development*, 9(4), 298–312.

Tacoli, C. 2011 *Not only climate change: Mobility, vulnerability and socio-economic transformation in environmentally fragile areas of Bolivia, Senegal and Tanzania*, Human Settlements Working Paper Series; Rural-Urban Interactions and Livelihood Strategies.

UN Population Division 2015 *World population prospects*. esa.un.org.

UNESCO-UIS 2012 *Adult and youth literacy, 1990–2015: Analysis of data for 41 selected countries*. UNESCO Institute for Statistics.

van der Geest, K. 2009 *Ghana: Case study report*. Environmental Change and Forced Migration Scenarios (EACH-FOR) Project.

van der Land, V. and Hummel, D. 2013 "Vulnerability and the role of education in environmentally induced migration in Mali and Senegal" *Ecology and Society*, 18(4), 14.

Van Hear, N. 2010 "Theories of migration and social change" *Journal of Ethnic and Migration Studies*, 36(10), 1531–1536.

8 A migrant typology

Different types of migrants

A migrant typology aims at categorising different types of migrants based on selected criteria. It helps identify those whose migration is influenced by climate change and environmental stress and consequently develop specific measures to respond to those in need. The present migrant typology has been developed on the basis of findings from qualitative data based on research from rural Mali and Senegal. The interviewed migrants have been grouped along the following characteristics: socio-demographic aspects (e.g. age, gender, family status and the level of education), the duration and destination of migration, the motives of migration and the impact of environmental factors on migration. The different types of migrants have been identified in a way that their traits are the most homogenous within a group but differ sufficiently compared to other migrant types (Strauss 1991; Kluge 2000; Kelle and Kluge 2010). This technique resulted in a classification of seven types of migrants from rural areas in the West African Sahel. One of the main differentiating factors is the influence of the environment on each type of migrant and the character of their migration, either voluntary to forced (see Table 8.1).

The seven types of migrants identified are: 1) the *Well-Educated*, 2) the *Adventurous*, 3) the *Ambitious*, 4) the *Transformer*, 5) the *Supplementers* and 6) the *Deprived* and 7) the *Trapped*. Type 7, however, does not characterise a specific type of migrant but describes a group of people that is not able to migrate even though they may want to leave. This group is therefore not included in Table 8.1.

Type 1 – the Well-Educated

The *Well-Educated* migrants are young people with a secondary education who leave the rural areas to pursue their studies. Their main migration motive is to achieve a higher education or a better vocational training. Adventure, curiosity, desire for an urban lifestyle and/or independence from their parents are often secondary motives for their migration. Environmental factors, on the contrary, play no role in their decision to leave. The *Well-Educated* are mainly 18 years old and single. Young men still dominate this group because the level of formal schooling of boys is usually higher than of girls. In contrast, girls in rural areas are still often expected to marry and fulfil the traditional role of a married woman in

Table 8.1 Typology of migrants by impact of environmental factors and the character of their migration.

Character of migration	Impact of environmental factors on migration		
	None	*Weak*	*Strong*
Voluntary	Type 1 The Well-Educated Type 2 The Adventurous	Type 3 The Ambitious Type 4 The Transformers Type 5 The Supplementers	
Forced			Type 6 The Deprived

Source: Author.

the household even after having successfully finished secondary school. Nevertheless, the number of girls with a high level of formal education has increased in both countries and is likely to continue in the future.

The *Well-Educated* do not come from the poorest families because they need to be able to pay for the costs and fees related to schooling and university, and at the same time, be able to compensate for a household member that does not contribute to the family's livelihood, either by working in agriculture or by supporting the family back home with remittances. Young people who leave the rural areas to pursue their education usually migrate to the capital or big cities within the country or, to a far lesser extent, to cities in neighbouring countries. Their migration is primarily voluntary in character, albeit young scholars often have to leave to bigger cities because there are usually no opportunities to pursue their studies in the rural areas or in nearby towns. The choice of destination depends on the availability of a university where they are able to continue their studies or on the availability and potential for better vocational training opportunities than those offered in the rural areas. They often have family or community members in the city of destination with whom they usually stay with – at least during the first weeks or months. Friends or family in the destination area give the migrant time to search for accommodation, jobs and adapt to the city life.

Most people who belong to this group of migrants will leave the rural areas long term or permanently. Most of the *Well-Educated* will be employed in the cities and many prefer the urban lifestyle that they have adapted to during their studies and which they do not want to give up. However, for those who would like to return to their area of origin, it would be difficult to find adequate employment in the rural areas after finishing their studies. Thus, the *Well-Educated* only return to the rural area to visit the family in the village and support them financially. A typical example for this type of migrant is Yacouba, a student from a Malian village (see Box 6.4). Today, the general level of education is still low in both rural areas, but the number of boys and girl from rural areas attending secondary schools and universities is increasing. Therefore, it seems very likely that this type of migrant will gain greater importance in the future. Table 8.2 provides a detailed description of the different types of migrants.

Table 8.2 Characterization of the different types of migrants.

	Type 1 The Well-Educated	Type 2 The Adventurous	Type 3 The Ambitious	Type 4 The Transformers	Type 5 The Supplementers	Type 6 The Deprived	Type 7 The Trapped
Age	16–20	14–25	18–35	16–35	25–50	30 upwards	14 upwards
Gender	primarily men, increasingly women	both young men and women	primarily men	primarily men	primarily men	primarily men	primarily women
Education	secondary education	none or primary education	primary or secondary education	none or primary education	none or primary education	none or primary education	none or primary education
Marital status	single	single	single or married	single or married	single or married	married	single or married
Economic activity	student or apprentice	temporary occasional jobs	own business or temporary jobs	petty trade/ business or employee	farming in combination with temporary jobs	temporary jobs	farming or housemaid
Migration destination	capital	urban areas within the country or neighbouring countries	capital, economic centres in the country, in the region or international	urban areas in the country or neighbouring countries	within the country or to a lesser extent to neighbouring countries	rural or urban areas within the country	`
Migration duration	long-term or permanent	short- or long-term	long-term	long-term	seasonal	long-term	`
Main motivation for migration	education or vocational training	adventure, independence, financial autonomy	money, success and social prestige	employment other than agriculture	food security and economic gains	food security	`
Impact of environment on migration decision	none	none	low	low	low or high	high	none or high

Source: Author.

Type 2 – the Adventurous

The *Adventurous* leave the rural areas with the desire to experience what is described as "faire la jeunesse" (enjoying youth). The migration motives of the *Adventurous* are manifold and include economic independence, autonomy from parents and social control of the village, the desire for consumer goods, curiosity to discover the world outside their village and adventure. They are usually girls/young women and boys/young men between the ages of 14 and 25 years who are not yet married. The level of education of the *Adventurous* spans from no formal schooling to primary or secondary level education. The lower the level of education, the younger the migrants when they first leave the village. A higher level of education decreases the likelihood of girls and boys migrating at a young age. Some adolescents, however, abandon school at a secondary education level in order to leave the rural area. For boys, this first migration can often constitutes a rite of passage from boy to manhood.

For both girls and boys migration is often a trend among peers that increases the will, but also the pressure to migrate. A competition among peers over things that are not available or not easy to achieve in the rural areas encourages the migration of the *Adventurous*. This includes the competition for modern clothes, haircuts, jewellery and kitchen equipment – which all together make them a more appealing candidate for marriage. It also includes other goods, such as mobile phones, but also for skills, such as learning another language or a more sophisticated cuisine. In areas where arranged marriage is still a common custom, migration also constitutes an opportunity to postpone or avoid arranged marriage. While migration for adventure has become a trend among today's youth, the first migrants or pioneer migrants who left the rural areas mainly belonged to the group of the *Adventurous*.

Today some communities still do not approve of young people, especially young women, leaving the rural areas and becoming independent. Therefore, boys and girls either leave secretly or argue that they will leave in order to support the household financially. They may use the lack of financial means however, as a justification of migration for other more individual reasons. Environmental stress hardly plays any role in the decision of the *Adventurous* to migrate. Nevertheless, their income gained in migration might be partly used to support the household. Their migration is primarily voluntary in character, but peer pressure may strongly influence their migration.

The *Adventurous* usually migrate to urban areas within the country or to neighbouring countries where they work in temporary occasional jobs. While young women rather stay in the country, men – particularly from Mali – often migrate across borders. Today destinations outside the African continent are rarely chosen by this group due to the high risks and costs and usually require a sudden opportunity or a friend that encourages them to come along. Many of these migrants rely on social networks built by elder brothers or sisters, friends or other family or community members. The social network facilitates their accommodation and job search; however, it is not a prerequisite for their migration. The duration of their migration differs between a few months and a couple of years. If they found a relatively well-paid job, they usually enjoy the urban lifestyle and newly gained independence and stay for a longer period of time. Migration often takes place in different turns over several years. It is common for this type of migrant to return to the village for some time only to leave again for a second, third or fourth time, either to the same or a different destination. Most of the *Adventurous* return eventually to the rural areas – often for marriage – and centre their life in the village or a nearby town. An example for an *Adventurous* migrant is Malik (see Box 6.1). Even though this type of migrant may be dominant among young people today, its importance is likely to decrease in the future. An increasing level of education favours the *Well-Educated* migrants instead.

Type 3 – the Ambitious

The *Ambitious* migrants have a strong goal for their migration: economic success. This includes the desire for a higher social standing and to realise a lifestyle that differs from common villagers. Thus, money, investments, consumer goods and the related prestige are very important for this type of migrant. Aware that small-scale agriculture will not allow them to realise their goal, the *Ambitious* may migrate to find better employment opportunities elsewhere. Although their migration may be initially driven by a lack of financial means in the household due to increasingly unfavourable agricultural conditions, environmental factors only play a small role for their migration. They acknowledge that agriculture will never fulfil their goals; therefore, their migration is primarily voluntary in character. The *Ambitious* are young to middle-aged people, mainly between 18 and 35 years old and primarily men. Depending on their age, they are either single or married. They usually have a formal education at the primary and secondary level. Although they are aware that basic education is necessary to achieve their goals, some of them leave secondary school before graduation, in order to start earning money as soon as possible. The *Ambitious* migrants are very hardworking, mainly in trades, factories or handicrafts. They often start at a low-level position and work their way up until they eventually create their own business. Most of them restrain themselves to a very simple lifestyle in order to save up money for their own business, investments and family back home.

The *Ambitious* tend to migrate for a long period of time to distant destinations. They choose destinations where the expected gains are higher than destinations closer to home. Thus, their migration is usually directed to the economic capitals in the country or in neighbouring countries. Some of them even migrate to destinations outside the continent or aspire to eventually go to Europe where they expect a greater level of economic success than in other African countries. Whether they prefer to stay or to migrate does not matter because for this type of migrant, somebody who wants to become someone has to migrate to try one's luck. The *Ambitious* usually stay for several years or even decades in migration only returning for short visits to the village if afforded the time, money and legal status. Although they are absent for a large period of time, they usually maintain a strong connection to the rural areas. This is because wife/wives and children often remain in the rural areas and most of the money gained will be invested in the village. The remittances are not only used to increase the living standards and the social standing of the (absent) migrant and his family, but also to invest in housing, livestock and farming in the village. The *Ambitious* prefer to invest in rural areas where they get more for their money than they would in urban areas. At the same time, the migrants can showcase their success and improve their social standing in the community.

The *Ambitious* are often among the bravest, most physically fit and hardworking of a household or community, shouldering the hopes of the family and sometimes even of the village for financial support, improved living conditions and development. They are often the first in the family to migrate or to migrate to destinations outside the country. As a result, they inspire other household or community members to follow them to the destination area because of the potential to become equally successful. Aside from their own desire to succeed in life, they are also often confronted with a lot of pressure to fulfil the expectations of others and to send remittances or other proof of their success back home. The pressure increases if other family and/or community members have financially supported the migrant in order to realise the migration plan. This is particularly true among international migrants for whom it is difficult to return home. Those who have not been successful cannot return to the village empty-handed because of the perceived shame for the family. For those who have been successful, it is also difficult to return home for good because of family expectations to maintain the standard of living afforded by remittances.

Climate change and other stressors may worsen the conditions for agriculture and increase the need for the migrants to support the household financially; however, the initial motivation for the migration of the *Ambitious* – economic success – does not change. An example for this type of migrants is Moustapha, an international migrant from Senegal (see Box 6.5). The number of *Ambitious* migrants is still relatively small but is likely to grow in the future among men, and increasingly among women, with social change, access to media and globalisation. Due to few and often inadequate alternative employment opportunities in the country, and in the region, the *Ambitious* will leave to search for their luck in other parts of the world.

Type 4 – the Transformers

The *Transformers* usually migrate for money and employment and are fairly common in the West African Sahel. Due to their high numbers, they contribute to structural changes in the region, which include, for instance, the transformation from farming as traditional economic activity to traders or other jobs in the service sector as main economic activity. Therewith they become, although mainly unintentionally, *Transformers*. The *Transformers* are migrants who do not want to continue farming or who decide to look for other activities that may be more reliable and profitable than agriculture. Although they would prefer to stay in the rural areas if offered better employment opportunities, they are not averse to moving to other areas. They are usually not driven by a strong personal motive as compared to the *Ambitious*, but migrate in search for job opportunities outside of the agricultural sector.

Migrants of this type are primarily between 16 and 35 years old and are mostly men. The level of education is usually low with no or only primary education. Increasingly they have also started secondary school but rarely finish. Depending on their age, they are single or married with wife/wives and children either in the village and/or the destination area. The preferred destinations of the *Transformers* are urban areas within or in neighbouring countries where they usually stay for longer periods and migrate in rotation with siblings, or stay permanently. Their connection to the village usually degrades after years in migration, especially when their family lives in the destination area. This usually distinguishes them from the *Ambitious* who maintain strong relations to the rural areas. Nevertheless, some of these migrants aim to return to their village for retirement.

The degree of environmental factors that influence their migration decision varies. The lack of financial means of the household, often caused by increasingly unfavourable agricultural conditions, influences their decision to leave the rural areas. Oftentimes, especially in the early stage of their migration, they will financially support parents and siblings in the rural areas that will permit them to stay in the village. However, environmental factors are not the only, and often not the main driver of their migration. Population growth, in combination with limited access to additional fertile land, does not allow most young people to stay in the rural areas and gain their living through farming. Climate change may in addition to other factors limit the choice for many. The *Transformers*, however, do not want to continue agriculture but prefer to gain their living through petty trade, small business or as an employee, either at home or somewhere else. Their migration is of a primarily voluntary character because they aim either to not work as a farmer or to leave the rural areas. Thus, their migration decision and their capabilities fit their preferences and aspirations. This distinguishes them from the *Deprived* migrants (see below) who have to migrate, although they aspire to stay. In contrast to the *Ambitious*, the main migration motive of the *Transformers* is not necessarily economic success and better employment; they prefer a more reliable and more profitable employment in urban areas over agriculture. A *Transformer* could become an *Ambitious* migrant or the other way around. An example for this type of migrants is Aliou (see Box 6.2). The *Transformers* are common in the West African Sahel and are likely to increase in numbers in the future due to climate change, population growth and aspirations for a different lifestyle and a better future.

Type 5 – the Supplementers

The *Supplementers* are farmers who carry out another economic activity in migration to add to income generated through small-scale farming. Normally these migrants leave during the dry season, thus could also be called "seasonal migrants". During nine months of the dry season, when little work has to be done on the fields, they leave the rural area to work for a few months in temporary jobs, either in other rural or urban areas within the country or in neighbouring countries. Their main migration motive is thus to supplement their agricultural income with additional income from other sources. Since the alternative income opportunities on-site are often rare or poorly paid, they have to migrate to other areas in order to find temporary jobs. These migrants return after several months to harvest and continue their farming activities. The *Supplementers* are young to middle-aged male farmers, mainly between 25 to 50 years old. Some continue to migrate up to old age especially when they have no sons at a working age or their children are pursuing a higher education. The *Supplementers* usually have no or only a basic formal education. Most of them are married and family fathers.

Generally, the annual seasonal migration is a common habit among farmers who are *Supplementers*. Although some of the migrants aim at improving their livelihoods, they usually do not have higher ambitions related to the migration. Agriculture remains their main and preferred economic activity and their life is centred in the rural areas with their families. In contrast to the other types of migrants, the motive and the character of migration among *Supplementers* can differ between two migrants, but also for the same person over time. For some *Supplementers*, migration has a forced quality because they need to migrate in order to ensure the household's food security. This is particularly the case for the poorest migrants. The number of migrants that need to complement their income also increases in the years with poor yields. External stressors and a combination of other unfavourable factors may shift a migrant classified as a *Supplementer* to the last migration type: the *Deprived*. Others, however, choose to migrate to increase their household income and improve their livelihoods. This allows for investments and to cope with current and future external stress. Thus, their migration has a voluntary character.

Environmental stressors may influence their migration patterns by leaving earlier or staying longer in migration. The duration of the migration might vary between two and nine months depending on the need for additional income and other factors. In contrast to other migration types, however, it rarely takes longer. Climate change and environmental stress may also increase the need to migrate but rarely influences the decision to migrate itself. The seasonal migration not only allows farmers to cope with acute or future stress, but also to invest in livestock, seeds, fertiliser, farming equipment or housing. Moreover, migration also provides the opportunity to bring goods, food and equipment to the village that is not available or only available at a higher price in the rural areas. An example for this type of migrants is Elhadj (see Box 5.2). Today, the *Supplementers* are still one of the most common forms of migration in the West African Sahel. However, increasing education, population growth and long-term rural-urban migration are likely to reduce the importance of this type of migrants in the future.

Type 6 – the Deprived

The *Deprived* migrants have no other choice but to migrate. Often the poorest in the society, the *Deprived* and their families are highly vulnerable to environmental and other external stressors. Driven by the need to ensure their families' food security, they give up farming as their main activity and try to gain the money needed during migration. Environmental stressors, such as unreliable rainfall, degraded soils or losses of yields, play a major role in their migration decision. In most cases, it is not only the environmental stressor, but a combination of unfavourable factors such as poor yields and a lack of financial means for investments alongside poor socio-economic conditions that force the *Deprived* to give up farming and leave. In contrast to the *Supplementers*, the *Deprived* have to give up their farming activities because seasonal migration alone no longer allows them to ensure their household's livelihood. The *Deprived* are forced to migrate for a longer period or even permanently to work in casual, poorly paid jobs to ensure the family's livelihood. They would prefer to stay in the rural areas to farm, but financial restrictions prevent them from doing so.

The *Deprived* migrants are usually middle-aged male farmers, 30 years old and upward, with none or little formal education. They are often married and have small children. In most cases they are the only male family member at a working age – often the head of the household – and thus highly responsible for other family members. While the *Deprived* migrants need to stay in migration, their families – usually women, small children and elders – remain in the village and continue farming at a very limited level. They heavily depend on the migrant's financial support to ensure their livelihoods. This type of migrant typically chooses urban or rural destinations within the country and, to a lower extent, migrates to neighbouring countries.

In contrast to the *Supplementers* and the *Ambitious* migrants, there is no other ambition linked to their migration apart from survival and in contrast to the *Transformers*, the *Deprived* usually have no alternative than to leave agriculture in order to ensure their family's livelihoods. Describing this type of migration as an adaptation strategy would be euphemistic because there is little or no agency involved in their migration. It should thus be considered "forced migration." Examples for this type of migrants are Moussa (see Box 5.1) who needs to ensure the food security of his mother and sister, or Ndaga who migrated during the severe droughts in the 1980s. The *Deprived* migrants have been rare in the two rural study areas. Climate change may increase this type of migration in the future if more people are unable to ensure their households' food security by supplementing the yields with income from seasonal migration due to worsening climatic conditions.

Type 7 – the Trapped

Lastly, there are people in the rural areas of the West African Sahel who do not have the capability to migrate even if they want. This group does not contain migrants, but "trapped populations" who do not have the financial means to migrate or are forced to stay due to social norms. People who did not have the financial means to migrate were rare in the rural study areas. While the group of the *Deprived* migrants is unable to stay in the rural areas to continue farming activities, the *Trapped* are deprived of leaving the rural areas. The *Trapped* are primarily women of all ages with no formal education or only at a primary level. In the West African Sahel, women are often restricted in their decision to migrate: married women cannot leave the area without the permission of their husbands and young unmarried women need the approval of their fathers and the community to leave. Social norms thus determine the capability to migrate, particularly for women.

The majority of the girls and women from the rural areas originate from farming households and thus strongly depend on the natural environment. They often have no or little income from small trading activities and few opportunities to improve their livelihoods by themselves. Due to their restrictions, the *Trapped* are particularly vulnerable to environmental or other external stressors. Since the income-generating activities on-site are limited, women often strongly depend on the male household members and their remittances from migration. Just as the *Deprived* migrants do not choose to migrate, the *Trapped* do not choose to stay. Little or no agency is involved in the decision to stay and thus it is of a forced character. Depriving these women from migration also means depriving them from achieving greater autonomy, economic independence, experience and a life education. An example for this type of migrants is Binta (see Box 5.3) and many other women, particularly from the Malian study area.

Environmental reasons may play a role for those who do not have the financial means to leave the area. Although the numbers were very low in the study areas, climate change may increase this type of non-migrants in the future. Nevertheless, most people in this group are deprived of migration due to traditional social norms and gender roles, not to environmental stress. Increasing pressure on the households' food security caused by environmental stress may indeed increase the need to migrate for women in order to subsidise the household's income and in turn, contribute to changes in gender roles that could eventually abolish their deprivation from migrating.

The typology and the concept of "environmental migrants"

The typology illustrates that the migrants and their reasons and motives to migrate vary strongly, even in a region with a harsh environment like the West African Sahel. Nevertheless, studies on the environment-migration research that focus on the region tend to assume that the majority of the people migrate for environmental reasons and are thus *environmental migrants*. The research for this book and the typology show, however, that environmental factors are not the main driver of migration for many people. So, who are the often-cited *environmental migrants*?

There is no commonly agreed definition. Considering the often-cited, yet broad IOM definition of *environmental migrants* (IOM 2007: 1), only two groups of this present typology fulfil the criteria: the *Supplementers* and the *Deprived* migrants. The migration of the first three types of migrants – the *Well-Educated*, the *Adventurous* and the *Ambitious* – is characterised by the wish to realise a strong personal goal and individual aspiration. Moreover, they do have the capability to decide whether to migrate or not out of free will. Environmental changes play no role or a minor role in their migration decision. For the *Transformers*, the food security and livelihood situation of the household may influence the migration decision to differing degrees. Nevertheless, it is still their preference for an urban life or an activity outside the agricultural sector and not environmental stress that pushes them to leave the rural areas. In contrast, the migration decision of the *Supplementers* and the *Deprived* migrants is influenced by environmental factors, although to different degrees. Those *Supplementers* who primarily migrate to improve their livelihoods may only be driven by environmental conditions in the area, such as the seasonality of rainfalls. The impact of environmental stressors on migration is higher for those who need to migrate to supplement their income in order to ensure the households' food security. In both cases, the seasonal migration of the *Supplementers* is a common habit and contributes to cope with current and future stress. The impact of environmental stressors on the *Deprived* is usually very strong and forces them to migrate. In most cases it is unfavourable socio-economic conditions that set the stage for the damage environmental stress (may) cause.

The degree of voluntariness or the capability to decide between staying and migrating also differs between the groups. While the *Supplementers* are able to decide between migrating and staying as well as the duration of their migration period, the *Deprived* and the *Trapped*, have little or no capability to decide on whether to migrate or not. The migration of the *Supplementers* may be described as a livelihood or adaptation strategy. In contrast, the migration of *Deprived* contains no agency but is rather a consequence of a failure of adaptation to environmental stressors in the region. Those who do not have the capability to choose freely between migrating and staying are the most disadvantaged people because they are least likely to live the lives they value and have either a high level of responsibility or are highly dependent on other household members.

The categorisation of the migrants from one type to another can change over time depending on the social, economic and environmental conditions. While somebody may have migrated for curiosity and adventure at a young age and thus would have been classified as an *Adventurous* migrant, that same person may become a *Supplementer* after having funded the family. The same migrant may even become either *Deprived* or *Trapped*. Future research should thus consider the broad variety of differing capabilities and aspirations to migrate and stay in the region, keeping in mind that those who may not migrate today for environmental reasons may do so tomorrow, or vice versa.

Bibliography

IOM 2007 *Discussion note: migration and the environment* (Ninety-fourth Session, MC/INF/288), International Organization for Migration (IOM).

Kelle, U. and Kluge, S. 2010 *Vom Einzelfall zum Typus. Fallvergleich und Fallkontrastierung in der qualitativen Sozialforschung*, Wiesbaden: VS Verl. für Sozialwiss.

Kluge, S. 2000 "Empirisch begründete Typenbildung in der qualitativen Sozialforschung" *Forum Qualitative Sozialforschung*, 1(1), Art. 14.

Strauss, A.L. 1991 *Grundlagen qualitativer Sozialforschung: Datenanalyse und Theoriebildung in der empirischen soziologischen Forschung* (Übergänge, 10), München: Fink.

9 Migration in the "global North" and the "global South"

Different notions of migration in the "global North" and "global South"

Migration is a global phenomenon, present in all societies all over the world. It has been a normal aspect of social life and social change throughout history (Castles 2010). Nevertheless, it is often assessed differently for the "North" and the "South". Mobility in the "global North" is usually regarded as a sign of individual progress and an expression of a modern society and is thus perceived as desirable, while mobility in the "global South" is often depicted as a symptom of failure and as such it is presumed that it has to be prevented.

These differing notions of migration may result from a categorisation in politics and research that divides the world into two different parts, labelled as the "global North" and the "global South" or "developed" and "developing" world or countries. The "global North" and "South" describe the socio-economic division of the world with the wealthy countries primarily located in the northern hemisphere and poor countries mainly located in the southern hemisphere. According to the United Nations, the "Northern world" comprises all of Europe and Northern America along with Japan, Australia and New Zealand, while all other countries are classified as "developing countries". The "North" is characterised by economic development and manufacturing industry, political stability and a functioning education system and its population has enough food and shelter. The "South" in contrast is characterised by lacking economic development and technologies, political instability and its population generally does not have enough food and shelter. Based on this division, which has been described as "intellectually lazy" because countries should be classified more precisely (The World Bank 2016), either part of the world is usually linked to specific associations and prejudices. This in turn may contribute to a view of a potentially similar phenomenon in a different light in either part of the world.

Migration is often considered differently in the "North" and in the "South". Research on migration in the "global South" usually focuses on the reasons for mobility, assuming that people need to leave a certain area. Mobility is thus considered as not desirable and as something that should be prevented. This sedentary perspective on migration, which focuses on the reasons that cause people to leave, has the tendency to understand mobility as an exception rather than as normal (Klute and Hahn 2007). That has been criticised by various scholars. De Haan for instance states that the "views about migration and migrants [in development studies, author] are often based on an assumption of sedentarism, that populations used to be immobile and have been uprooted by economic or environmental forces. There is however much evidence to challenge this sedentary bias, and to view population movement as the norm rather than the exception" (de Haan 1999: 7). Indeed, considering the high mobility in many parts of Africa, the opposite would make more sense (de Bruijn et al. 2001). The empirical research for this book has also shown that over 80% of the surveyed population in rural Mali and Senegal had personal migration experience, suggesting that mobility is the norm rather than an exception.

Today it seems acknowledged that labour migration between and within rural and urban areas is a central element in the livelihoods of many rural households in developing countries and thus is a "normal" element of their society (de Haan 1999). Moreover, studies have shown that the migrant's remittances from international migration contribute considerably to the development in the home communities and countries. The amount of remittances is often higher than Overseas Development Assistance or Foreign Direct Investment. Research on the migration and development nexus has highlighted the benefits of migration for development in the "South". Nevertheless, the view on migration has not changed considerably in research and development practice. For the latter, Bakewell argues that development practice continues to aim at controlling and reducing mobility by improving living conditions in the sending areas, while development theory has for a long time acknowledged that migration is crucial for development in rural areas. He describes this gap between development theory and development practice as "sedentary bias" (Bakewell 2008). Moreover, research has shown that people may not be willing to stay in the sending areas, even though conditions improve. Quite the contrary, migration flows usually increase with further development because people have more financial means to travel and more options (de Haas 2010). Thus, better living conditions in the rural areas may not restrain people from migrating, even though it may reduce the need to migrate for some.

The underlying assumption that development enables people to stay remains prominent and research studies and development practice continue to frame migration as a desperate move to escape poverty or as a response to crisis (Bakewell and de Haas 2007; Hahn and Klute 2007; Bakewell 2008). This is also the case for research on the linkages between climate change, environment and migration, which has only to a limited extend applied the knowledge of related fields. Countries in the "North" tend to perceive international migration from the "South" as a flight from their country, which may trigger fears of a potential invasion. This in turn leads to strict visa policies, repressive border control and/ or activities to address the "root causes" of migration in the countries of origin in order to prevent these movements and make mobility highly selective (Castles 2010). Although freedom of movement is a human right, according to Article 13 of the Universal Declaration of Human Rights, most people from the "South" have no access to free movement across international borders because they lack either the economic resources or the political rights to do so. At the same time, for people from the "North", international migration and free movement is a matter of course.

Mobility in the "global North" in contrast to mobility in the "South" is celebrated as individual progress and liberty as well as an expression of a modern open society (Castles 2010). In Western countries the mobility discourse is shaped by the opinion that to be modern means to be mobile (Bauman 1994). Being mobile is considered a fundamental part of modernity, and spatial mobility an expression of this approach (Tully and Baier 2006). Industrialisation led to an increasing differentiation of functions and the connection to places. While in the past almost all activities of a family occurred in one place, today living, education, employment or leisure activities often take place at different locations and require being mobile. Technological progress and increasing mobility infrastructure have also contributed to a mobile society (Tully and Baier 2006).

Today, mobility of young people in "Northern" countries from rural areas to urban agglomerations or across countries and continents is strongly encouraged. It is considered a rational decision to improve one's education and/or employment, to increase income or for personal development, rather than to flee from economic hardship. The rural exodus of young people in the "North" for individual purposes, such as studies, professional reasons, marriage or lifestyle is commonly acknowledged and has become the norm. Modern transportation, technology and culture further encourage international migration. Thinking and moving beyond borders has become a common habit and a sign of modernity in Western societies (Urry 2007). Mobility in the "North" is considered an intrinsic want, an activity that generates identities and expresses a certain lifestyle. Moreover, national or multinational policy-programs encourage the mobility of people across the European Union (EU) and all over the world. The successful "Erasmus" education programme of the European Union for instance has facilitated the mobility of about 3 million students across EU member states. One aim of the programme is the creation of European identities (Maiworm and Over 2013). All in all, mobility in the "North" is "the badge of a modern open society" (Castles 2010: 1567) and thus viewed positively.

The idea of a good life and its impact on the environment-migration research

Research on the environment-migration nexus has incorporated the general view on migration in the "South" as a result of poverty and external stressors, focussing on environmental stress as its main cause. Although the view on migration from areas affected by environmental degradation has changed during the last decades, it still represents a sedentary perspective. Indeed, research considers mobility not anymore primarily as population displacements caused by environmental stress, but as a coping or adaptation strategy to acute or future stress. Nevertheless, this perspective still presumes that people need to leave in order to adapt to stress. Migration as a livelihood activity not only eases pressure to better cope with environmental stress, but also aims at improving the household's livelihood and economic well-being (Ellis 2003).

Studies on the linkages of environmental factors and migration in the West African Sahel, however, often assume that it is mainly environmental stress that leads people to migrate, without actually considering other reasons for migration (van der Land et al. forthcoming). Assuming that it is only or primarily environmental reasons that cause people to leave, studies already determine the perspective of migration as a need to migrate from the respective study area. Studies often only inquire about the type of environmental factors that encourages migration, without considering that other reasons may have been more relevant for the migration decision. This leads often to the use of questionable leading questions as a research method. This approach not only presumes that environmental factors primarily drive migration from the respective areas but also ignores that people may want to migrate in order to realise individual motives and aspirations, despite poor environmental conditions. Therewith, studies largely underestimate the role of individual motives and aspirations for migration in developing countries and from areas affected by slow-onset environmental changes.

This approach implies an underlying assumption – often applied in research in developing countries – that people in the "South" prefer to stay in their area of origin. At the same time, the "global North" itself strives for advancement and change through migration. These assumptions result from the differing notions of migration in the "North" and in the "South" and can be linked to the idea of "a good life" that often differs between researcher or development agencies and the migrants themselves. In order to overcome the "sedentary bias" between development research and practice, Bakewell (2008) has called for a reconsideration of the ideas of "a good life" envisaged in development initiatives, arguing that they often differ from the conceptions of "a good life" of the people with which they work. He suggests that development agencies aim to empower people in the "South" to achieve a better quality of life at "home", while the people themselves may relate an improved quality of life to new opportunities and to a new "home" elsewhere (Bakewell 2008).

Sen's Capability Approach and his understanding of development as freedom incorporates the individual's choice for a good life (see Chapter 3). Sen understands development as expanding people's capabilities to lead a good life. What matters is what people are effectively able to do and to be in order to realise lives they value and have reason to value (Sen 2000). An individual decision does not only depend on the available options, thus on one's capability set, but also on one's preferences for an option. With respect to mobility, the understanding of development as expanding individual capabilities relates to the choice to migrate and stay and to realise a good life either at home or elsewhere. The sedentary perspective in research and the focus on the potential causes of migration in the sending areas prevent scholars from considering that people actually may prefer to migrate. Acknowledging the individual's idea of and choice for a good life may help to understand that people in the "South" may also desire to migrate either to earn their living elsewhere in order to realise a better life back home or to leave the rural areas in order to realise a good life elsewhere. Research, however, often ignores that migration can be a means to contribute to development in the sending areas, which in turn enlarges the individual choices for a good life at home or elsewhere.

In research on the environment-migration nexus, the idea of "a good life" may also differ between researchers – usually from the "global North" – and the people from the respective rural research areas in the West African Sahel and influence the findings. The understanding of migration as an adaptation strategy implies – if at all – only the aspect of improving living conditions back home, but does not include the idea of migration as a means to realise a good life elsewhere. The assumption that people in areas affected by climate change or environmental degradation wish to stay in the area and to continue subsistence agriculture often guide research and are thus a major obstacle to advancements in the field of environmental change and migration. The research for this book shows, however, that many young people do not see their future in the rural areas, either because access to fertile land is limited and unreliable climate condition make farming less attractive or because they imagine their future differently from their parents' way of life and different to subsistence agriculture. Research on migration from environmentally fragile areas in the "South" usually ignores that people may simply not want to stay in the rural areas and to continue agriculture but prefer to migrate. Lifestyle migration of young people motivated by individual aspirations seems not to fit the image that researchers often have of migrants from environmentally fragile environments, but in contrast seems obvious when analysing migration of young people in the "North".

The differing notions on the idea of a good life and migration in the "South" and in the "North" may result in misleading conclusions in research and development practice. Although migration motives may generally not differ as much as assumed between "North" and "South", the need to migrate is certainly more frequent in the "South". Higher levels of poverty and a greater dependency of people's livelihoods on agriculture may deter people from the "South" to choose between migrating and staying in order to realise what they consider a good life. However, life as a subsistence farmer in the West African Sahel or elsewhere in the world is not only arduous and may become more difficult with worsening climate conditions, it also offers few chances of livelihood improvements for young people and further generations. Young people in the "South" thus migrate not necessarily due to environmental and economic stress, but also for non-economic and individual migration motives in order to realise their aspirations, just as they do in the "North". Research should consider people's ideas of a good life and apply the same standards for migration in the "North" and in the "South" in order to avoid misleading conclusions. After all, migration motives of young people from rural areas in the "South" may not differ that much from those of their counterparts in the "North".

Types of migrants in the West African Sahel and in the "North"

The notions of migration differ between the "North" and the "South", but in what way does migration in the "North" really differ from mobility in the West African Sahel? In order to find out how migration in the "North" differs or relates to mobility in the "South", the types of migrants identified from research in rural Mali and Senegal (see Chapter 8) will be compared to (potential) similar types of migrants in Europe. The comparison, however, is only partly based on empirical evidence and thus, rather a thought experiment. A comparison of migration in Europe, which shall represent the "North" and the West African Sahel, as example for the "South" based on empirical evidence would go beyond the scope of this book, but may be an interesting endeavour for further research. The thought experiment aims to identify whether migration indeed differs considerably between the "North" and the "South" or whether the differences are based on differing notions of migration resulting from the sedentary perspective applied to migration in the "South".

Type 1 – the Well-Educated – more common in the "North"

The *Well-Educated* migrants exist in Europe as in the West African Sahel. This type of migrant is however more common in the "North" due to higher levels of education compared to the West African Sahel.

The literacy rate and particularly the rate of higher education in the West African Sahel are still low. In 2015, the gross enrolment in secondary education was on average at 113% in the EU, while it was 41% (2015) in Mali and 50% (2015) in Senegal (The World Bank 2017). Gross enrolment of ratios greater than 100% can be caused by students whose age exceeds the official age group (e.g. by late enrolment, early enrolment, or repetition). The enrolment in tertiary education is on average at 68% in the EU, while it is only 7% (2012) in Mali and 10% (2015) in Senegal (The World Bank 2017). Although tertiary enrolment is still low in Mali and Senegal compared to the EU, enrolment has more than tripled since the year 2000 in both countries.

Tertiary education all over the world is usually only available in cities and not in rural areas. Young people from rural areas from both the "North" and the "South" thus need to move to a city in order to continue their studies at university. Although the costs of higher education vary between Western countries, a university enrolment usually is affordable in most European countries and students often have the possibility to receive scholarships to cover the costs of their studies. In contrast, many people from rural areas in the West African Sahel cannot afford accommodation in the university cities and often lack financial means to pay fees and material needed to pursue a higher education. Apart from that a good quality education is often only available abroad or in an expensive private university, which seems out of reach for many.

Primary and secondary education is compulsory in most countries. Nevertheless, many children in the West African Sahel do not attend school because there is no school in an acceptable distance or because parents prefer them to help on the fields. In contrast in Europe, schooling infrastructure is usually much better and not sending the children to school is sanctioned. This guarantees that most children are literate and do have a secondary education, which provides them with the ability to choose a tertiary education at a later point of time, if wanted. Moreover, education has become a common value in Western countries, while households in development countries may not (yet) appraise the benefits of education for their children in the same way. The children's labour force is often needed to contribute to the household's income and food security and thus considered more valuable than education.

The *Well-Educated* leave the rural areas in the West African Sahel for better educational, vocational and professional perspectives – as do their counterparts in the "North". Although the *Well-Educated* migrants are more common in the "North" due to higher levels of education, the increasing level of schooling and education in Mali and Senegal suggests that this type of migrant will also increase in the West African Sahel in the future.

Type 2 – the Adventurous – greater freedom to move in the "North"

Young people all over the world migrate in search for adventure, desiring to discover the world outside their village, town, city or country and to meet new people. Rural exodus is a common phenomenon in both "global North" and "South", but it is more frequently accompanied by a certain need to support the household financially in the "South".

Capital cities in Europe often attract young and middle-aged adults due to greater opportunities for higher education and employment offered. The share of persons aged 20–54 in the total population peaked in the Danish capital of København, at 62 % (compared with a national average of 46% in 2013). In 2012, the younger and middle-aged adult populations of Amsterdam and Helsinki accounted for between 7 and 8 percentage points more of the total population than their respective national averages, while the difference in Sofia was almost 6 percentage points. Other big cities with a young age structure were Dublin and London, Ankara, Istanbul and Izmir in Turkey and the Norwegian capital of Oslo (Eurostat 2015).

The German capital Berlin for instance has in recent years attracted a number of young people that want to experience Berlin city life and often make their living with occasional jobs. The age group of the 20 to 25 year old is the biggest in the city and most young people live in the city centre districts, where the average age of inhabitants was lowest at less than 40 years (Statistik-bbb 2017). In Europe, the *Adventurous* migrants are usually in their twenties, while in Mali and Senegal people started to migrate already in their teens. The age difference results from the lower average number of years of formal schooling completed in the "South" compared to the "North", since this type usually migrates after school or vocational training. Young people in Europe usually attend school for a longer period of time than those in the West African Sahel and are thus older when migrating.

One major difference between the *Adventurous* migrants from Europe and from the West African Sahel is that migration in the latter region is often accompanied by a certain need to financially support the family. In the "North" young people usually migrate only out of free will and pleasure and may also be supported financially by their parents. In contrast to the *Supplementers*, however, the aspects of adventure and curiosity outweigh the need to support the family back home. In addition to the availability of financial means, the ability of choosing a destination differs between young people from the West African Sahel and their counterparts from the "North". West African countries – as the European countries in the EU – are organised in the Economic Community of West African States (ECOWAS), which warrants free movement of persons, goods and services. Nevertheless, the choice for international destinations across the African continent are limited for most people from rural West Africa due to financial resources and visa restrictions. Their curiosity to discover the outside world is thus mainly limited by external restrictions to the African continent and affect primarily the *Adventurous* and the *Ambitious* migrants. People from the "North", in contrast, may have more financial means and, at least theoretically, a greater freedom to move anywhere they want.

The *Adventurous* adapt an urban – and in West Africa often a "Western" lifestyle – that distinguishes themselves from friends and family in the rural areas. In the "North" the *Adventurous* are both male and female, while in the "South" this type of migrant is still primarily male. Nevertheless, the increasing feminisation of migration and changes of traditional gender roles in West Africa may increase the share of young women migrating for adventure in the future.

Type 3 – the Ambitious – success easier to realise in the "North"

The *Ambitious* migrants long for money and success and exist in the "North" and in the "South" alike. In the "South", however, there is a higher likelihood that the migration of the *Ambitious* is combined with a need to support the household financially than in the "North".

In both Europe and the West African Sahel, the *Ambitious* have an average level of education and come from average, middle-income homes and thus, are usually not the poorest in a community. In many cases their lives remain centred in their areas of origin, but they migrate for a temporary period for better employment and salaries elsewhere. One example for this type of migrant in Europe may be workers in assembly and construction, who agree to work for several weeks or months elsewhere for a higher salary. Better access to information on job opportunities via internet facilitate the search for employment and reduce the risk of migrating in Europe compared to West Africa, where migrants usually have to physically move in order to find employment opportunities elsewhere.

The money the *Ambitious* in "North" and "South" gain in migration allows them to increase savings and retirement provisions, provide for the family and to invest in housing and consumer goods, often in their area of origin. In migration, they often live under simple conditions in order to save money for themselves and their family back home. The understanding of "simple conditions" may however also differ between "North" and "South". In contrast to the *Adventurous*, the *Ambitious* are not or at least are less curious to get to know new places but focus on increasing their economic and social status. Therefore, the destination matters primarily with respect to the (expected) gains.

Type 4 – the Transformers – contribute to less profound changes in the "North"

The *Transformers* want to or have to leave the structurally weak rural areas in order to find (adequate) employment, in Europe and the West African Sahel alike, but have no higher ambitions related to their employment, like the *Ambitious* migrants. Nevertheless, the *Transformers* and the *Ambitious* resemble each other in several aspects that distinguishes them from their counterparts in the "North". In the "South" their migration for instance, can be accompanied by a certain need to support the family and they usually have to physically move in order to find employment opportunities elsewhere.

The *Transformers* in "North" and "South" migrate either for temporary periods and centre their lives in the rural area or move permanently to a destination that is mainly determined by employment opportunities. Migration patterns of those who do not stay permanently differ between "North" and "South". While in the "South" this type of migrant usually stays for several months in migration, only occasionally visiting the family back home, in European countries an increasing number of people move into cities and the phenomenon of commuters has also risen in recent years. In Germany, for instance, 60% of employees commuted to other municipalities and provinces in 2016. Weekly commuters, thus people who work and stay during the week in one location, but live during the weekends in another location with a partner or family, are common. The high number of commuters in Germany and in other European countries may be encouraged by a good transport infrastructure with well-developed highways, train and bus infrastructure for short and long distances, but also by a higher density of urban agglomerations than in the West African Sahel. Commuting may also become increasingly common in the "North" with higher ambitions and aspirations among men and women, who are juggling to combine a relationship or family and a professional career.

In the West African Sahel, leaving the rural areas means in most cases not to continue agriculture, the traditional economic activity of parents and ancestors. The migration of the younger generation into urban areas may thus contribute to major structural changes or transformations in society, and so they become, although mainly unintentionally, *Transformers*. In Europe, people no longer rely primarily on subsistence agriculture following industrialisation. It is thus less likely that this type of migrant contributes to profound changes in society in the "North". Nevertheless, the increasing number of commuters may also contribute to changes in social life and society. In the West African Sahel, an increasing pressure on people's land due to climate change and a high population growth, but also due to a high interest of young people to leave the rural areas may increase the number of the *Transformers* in the future.

Type 5 – the Supplementers – a phenomenon limited to the "South"

The *Supplementers* are probably the most typical type of migrants in the West African Sahel – or at least the type of migrants of which researchers think when talking about migration in the region. At the same time, this type of migrant hardly exists in the "North".

In the West African Sahel, 70-80% of the population depends on agriculture, mostly subsistence or small-scale farming. In contrast in the "North", subsistence farming hardly exists (anymore). In the past century, increased productivity through mechanisation and the use of fertilisers, selective breeding and effective pesticides and insecticides have changed agriculture from subsistence to intensive farming. In Germany, 60% of the population lived on farming at the beginning of the 20th century, while today it is only 3%. Today, a few farmers cultivate vast surfaces mainly for commercial purpose instead. Farmers in Germany, for instance, cultivated, according to the German farmers' association, about 58 hectares on average in 2012, while it was 4.5 hectares in Mali. In the European Union, farmers represent only less than 5% of the EU's working population. Yet, they manage nearly half of the EU's land area (EEA 2016).

As a result of different land inheritance laws from the beginning of the 20th century, farmers in northern Germany still cultivate bigger surfaces than farmers in the south of the country. While in the north only the eldest son inherited the entire land, in the south the surface had been divided among all inheritors. Some of the smaller farms complement their income from agriculture by other income sources, such as providing guestrooms, offering agricultural products in their own shop, providing leisure time activities (e.g. horse riding) etc. These supplemental activities of farmers in the "North", however, usually take place on-site and rarely include migration. In contrast to farmers in the "South", farmers from Western European countries do not migrate but often recruit seasonal labour from economically weaker neighbouring countries, for instance from Eastern European or Northern African countries, for the harvest of fruits (e.g. apples, strawberries or plums) or vegetables (e.g. asparagus, potatoes or cucumber).

Social trends in the West African Sahel, such as increasing education and the aspirations of young people to work and live in urban areas, may gradually decrease the number of the *Supplementers* in the future favouring the *Well-Educated* and the *Ambitious*. Worsening climate conditions may also contribute to *Supplementers* becoming *Deprived* migrants.

Type 6 – the Deprived and type 7 – the Trapped – more common in the "South" as a result of poverty

The *Deprived* migrants characterise people who have to leave their homes because they may not be able to earn a living, if they stay, although they would prefer to stay in their area of origin. This type of migrant exists primarily in the "South" due to increased poverty. It also exists in the "global North", but is rarely a matter of survival – at least in Northern and Central Europe.

In the "South", this type mainly applies to farmers who need to leave the rural areas and their agricultural activity because they are not able to ensure their own and the household's livelihoods through farming. In the "global North", this type of migrant may also exist but applies primarily to people who have to leave the structurally weak rural areas because they cannot find employment on-site or in a commuting distance. The difference between the *Deprived* and the *Transformers* is that the latter prefer or at least do not mind leaving, while the *Deprived* clearly would like to stay at "home" but are not able to do so. The main difference between *Deprived* migrants in the "North" and in the "South" is that migration of this type is closely linked to pure survival in the "South", while in the "North" social insurances usually prevent migration becoming a matter of survival.

The number of *Deprived* migrants seems to be low in both parts of the world. In the West African Sahel, they may either increase with worsening climate conditions due to the high dependency on farming or may decrease with increasing development.

In contrast to the *Deprived*, people characterised as *Trapped* are those who are not able to migrate, although they want to do so. While in the West African Sahel it includes primarily women, it is rare in the "global North".

In the West African Sahel, the *Trapped* people are primarily women deterred from leaving the rural areas by male family and community members, often based on and justified by traditional norms. The "trapped populations", thus, people living in environmentally fragile areas that do not have the financial means to migrate, would also fall under this category. In the "North", today it is rare that people do not have the ability to leave a certain area because it is not only commonly accepted, but also expected that young people – men and women – leave their home in order to build their future, i.e. to continue their education or to find employment.

Future climate change may restrain an increasing number of people from migrating in the West African Sahel as often assumed in literature. The findings for this book, however, suggest that climate change forces migrants to leave rather than to stay. With respect to the migration of women, current social trends, such as increasing education, feminisation of migration and the vanishing of traditional norms, may make the migration of women more likely and decrease the probability of being trapped for women in the West African Sahel.

Similarities and differences of migration in the "North" and "South"

The comparison of migration types identified for the West African Sahel with migrants in the "North" shows that some types of migrants exist in both parts of the world, while others only or mainly appear in the "South".

The first four types the *Well-Educated*, the *Adventurous*, the *Ambitious* and the *Transformers* are represented in both parts of the world. These types of migrants are particularly common among young people and imply a voluntary character of migration. Although the types of migrants are quite similar in Europe and the West African Sahel, there are slight differences between them resulting from the differing cultural, economic, natural and social conditions in both parts of the world. Despite the similarities, the migration of these types for instance is more likely to be accompanied by a certain need to support the household in the "South", while it is mainly a voluntary activity in the "North". In general, however, the migration motives of young people from rural areas in the West African Sahel seem not to differ that much from those of young people in the "North" – at least not in a way that the research suggests.

In contrast, the three remaining types of migration – the *Supplementers*, the *Deprived* and the *Trapped* – are mainly present in the West African Sahel, but rarely exist in Europe. The latter groups imply a certain need to migrate for the *Supplementers* and a forced character of migration for the *Deprived* and of staying for the *Trapped*. The *Supplementers* and the *Deprived* in the Sahel are mainly middle-aged farmers who are responsible for the livelihoods of their family.

Moreover, the distribution of the different types of migrants differs in the respective societies. The differences in distribution of migrants in the "North" and "South" may give a hint in which direction migration may develop in the West African Sahel. Type 1, the *Well-Educated* migrants, are much more common in the "North" than in the "South" due to a higher level of education in the "North". Increasing education in the West African Sahel may thus lead to higher numbers of *Well-Educated* migrants in the future. Type 2 (the *Adventurous*), Type 3 (the *Ambitious*) and Type 4 (the *Transformers*) may also increase in numbers in the Sahel in the future due to higher levels of education, high population growth and urbanisation as well as young people's retreat from agriculture. In contrast, Type 5, the *Supplementers*, and Type 7, the *Trapped*, may decrease for similar reasons. The number of Type 6, the *Deprived*, may change in either direction: on the one hand, climate change may increase the need for farmers to migrate, and on the other hand, increasing education and young people's retreat from agriculture may decrease the impact of environmental stress on people's migration.

Migration in the "global South" is often accompanied by a need or expectation and obligations from the household caused by poverty. Nevertheless, migration of young people in the "South" seems to be primarily voluntary and often motivated by aspirations for an urban lifestyle, curiosity or better educational or professional prospects – thus, by similar migration motives that encourage the mobility of young people in the "North". Both young people in the "North" AND in the "South" may see migration as one, or perhaps the only means to get ahead and to realise a good life. According to Richerson and Boyd, people all over the world who migrate voluntarily are mobile for a simple reason. "Most people migrate to improve their lot. Although their goals and aspirations vary, most prefer wealth to poverty, safety and security to fear and danger, health to illness, and equality to inequality" (Richerson and Boyd 2008: 877).

The focus of environment-migration research in the West African Sahel on people's needs and the assumption that people would prefer to stay in the rural areas working as subsistence farmers rather than earning their living with a more reliable and more profitable activity, ignores that people actually may want to migrate for different reasons. Research should thus stop analysing and considering migration differently in the "North" and in the "South" and overcome sedentary assumptions in research. The differences in migration between the "North" and "South" primarily result from the differing social-ecological conditions in the two regions. Chapter 7, however, has illustrated that social changes in the West African Sahel may have a considerable impact on migration motives and patterns and may also enlarge or diminish the differences in migration between "North" and "South". For a more profound understanding of the similarities and differences of mobility from the "North" and "South" further empirical research is needed. Particularly, young people often seem to have similar migration motives in both parts of the world. Assuming that young people in the Sahel only migrate in response to household needs caused by poverty and environmental stressors denies any form of agency and aspirations that may be related to their mobility.

Bibliography

Bakewell, O. 2008 "'Keeping them in their place': The ambivalent relationship between development and migration in Africa" *Third World Quarterly*, 29(7), 1341–1358.

Bakewell, O. and de Haas, H. 2007 "African migration: Continuities, discontinuities and recent transformation", in Chabal, P., Engel, U. and de Haan, L. eds. *African alternatives*, Leiden: Brill, 95–118.

Bauman, Z. 1994 "Parvenü und Paria: Helden und Opfer der Moderne" *Merkur*, 540, 237–248.

Castles, S. 2010 "Understanding global migration: a social transformation perspective" *Journal of Ethnic and Migration Studies*, 36(10), 1565–1586.

de Bruijn, M., van Dijk, R. and Foeken, D. 2001 "Mobile Africa: an introduction", in de Bruijn, M., van Dijk, R. and Foeken, D. eds. *Mobile Africa: Changing patterns of movement in Africa and beyond* (African dynamics, 1), Leiden: Brill, 1–7.

de Haan, A. 1999 "Livelihoods and poverty: The role of migration - a critical review of the migration literature" *Journal of Development Studies*, 36(2), 1–47.

de Haas, H. 2010 "Migration and development: a theoretical perspective" *International Migration Review*, 44(1), 227–264.

EEA 2016 *Agriculture*. European Environment Agency. eea.europa.eu.

Ellis, F. 2003 *A livelihood approach to migration and poverty reduction*. UK Department for International Development.

Eurostat 2015 *Statistics on European cities*. Eurostat. ec.europa.eu.

Hahn, H.P. and Klute, G. eds. 2007 *Cultures of migration: African perspectives*, Münster: Lit.

Klute, G. and Hahn, H.P. 2007 "Cultures of migration: introduction", in Hahn, H.P. and Klute, G. eds. *Cultures of migration: African perspectives*, Münster: Lit, 9–27.

Maiworm, F. and Over, A. 2013 *Studentische Mobilität und europäische Identität*. Bonn: Deutscher Akademischer Austauschdienst.

Richerson, P.J. and Boyd, R. 2008 "Migration: An engine for social change" *Nature*, 456(18), 877.

Sen, A. 2000 *Development as freedom*, New Delhi: Oxford University Press.

Statistik-bbb 2017 *Einwohnerinnen und Einwohner im Land Berlin am 31. Dezember 2016.* Amt für Statistik Berlin-Brandenburg.

Tully, C.J. and Baier, D. 2006 *Mobiler Alltag. Mobilität zwischen Option und Zwang. Vom Zusammenspiel biographischer Motive und sozialer Vorgaben,* Wiesbaden: VS Verlag für Sozialwissenschaften | GWV Fachverlage GmbH Wiesbaden.

Urry, J. 2007 *Mobilities,* Cambridge: Polity.

van der Land, V., Rómankiewicz, C. and van der Geest, K. forthcoming "Environment and migration – a review of West African case studies", in McLeman, R. and Gemenne, F. eds. *The Routledge handbook of environmental displacement and migration,* Routledge.

The World Bank 2016 *World development indicators 2016.* The World Bank. openknowledge.worldbank.org.

The World Bank 2017 *Data: Gross enrolement ratio.* The World Bank. data.worldbank.org.

10 Conclusion and outlook

Rethinking migration and environmental change in the West African Sahel

Contribution to a better understanding of the environment-migration nexus

Environmental stressors play a much smaller role than presumed in the migration decision from rural Mali and Senegal. Instead, migration motives are manifold and differ along age, gender and education. Young people migrate primarily to earn better educational and professional prospects, to fulfil their desire for consumer goods and an urban lifestyle, to gain economic independence from their parents and to fulfil their curiosity. Their migration motives echo those of young people in the "global North." It is individual aspirations that drive young people to leave the rural areas rather than the household's needs caused by environmental changes. Even if the migration of young people in the West African Sahel often is accompanied by a certain need to support the household, it is first and foremost their desire to fulfil their dreams and get ahead – just like their counterparts in the "North".

Environment-migration research claims to highlight people's agency by considering migration an active adaptation strategy to environmental stress. At the same time, it denies any form of self-determined agency by viewing migration as a household response to environmental stress and unfavourable conditions, ignoring non-economic reasons, individual motives and aspirations that may shape the migration decision. This may result from different notions of migration applied in research in the "global North" and in the "South". While migration is often assumed to be a desperate move to escape from poverty and/or environmental stress in the "South", it is considered an expression of modernity in the "North". Young people's migration in "Northern" countries from rural areas to urban agglomerations is strongly encouraged and considered a rational decision to improve education and/or employment as well as to increase income, rather than to flee economic hardship. At the same time, research in the "South" largely ignores the role of individual motives and aspirations for migration that may also stimulate migration from areas affected by environment stress. Moreover, this leads to the lack of consideration for any form of development and social changes within the geographical research areas and their societies. These social changes may, however, mitigate the impact of climate change on people's livelihoods and migration.

This book aimed to provide a better understanding of the linkages between slow-onset climate and environmental change and migration in the West African Sahel now and in the future. Its focus on individuals rather than on households has been vital to identify people's capabilities to choose between migrating and staying and their preferences and aspirations related to one or the other. This is crucial to distinguish whether people migrate or stay because they want to or because they need to do so. Moreover, it explains why people stay and others migrate from certain areas despite living under similar conditions. This book shows that in order to advance research on the linkages between environmental change and human mobility, it is vital to consider:

- the diversity of reasons and motives to migrate or to stay in areas affected by environmental changes, including opportunities elsewhere and non-economic motives;
- individual preferences and aspirations in addition to households' needs;
- people's capabilities to choose between migrating and staying in order to identify if people want or have to stay or to migrate;
- the local context and broader social transformation processes that can have a positive or negative influence on people's vulnerability to environmental stress;
- the different standards applied when analysing migration in the "global South" compared to mobility in the "North".

The theoretical and empirical analysis of the linkages between environmental changes and migration in the West African Sahel in this book takes into account these factors and finds the following key results:

- Environmental stress is rarely the main reason for migration, but if so, it particularly affects middle-aged male farmers with no formal education;
- Increasing level of education, urbanisation and changing lifestyles encourage young people to retreat from agriculture, irrespective of the conditions for farming. Thus, social changes may lessen the impact of climate change on people's livelihood and migration even if climate conditions worsen;
- Individual capabilities to choose between migrating and staying define the degree of voluntariness of the migration decision. The more likely people are to choose freely, the more individual preferences and aspirations determine the migration decision.

The next sections provide brief summaries of these main findings and conclude with policy recommendations based on findings from this research.

The relative importance of environmental reasons as main drivers of migration

The impact of climate change and environmental stress on people's livelihood and their migration in the West African Sahel is a major global concern. The high variability and lack of rainfall as the main environmental stressors threaten people's livelihoods that heavily depend on small-scale agriculture. Contrary to this conventional wisdom, empirical evidence from two rural areas in Mali and Senegal shows that environmental stress plays a much smaller role as a driver of migration than expected. It primarily affects the migration of middle-aged men with no or a low level of formal education. Men are traditionally responsible for their household's food security. Therefore, the need to migrate increases once they have founded a family. With no or a low level of formal education they have little prospects for well-paid non-agricultural employment.

Migration driven by environmental reasons is mainly short-term and to destinations within the country or to neighbouring countries. In times of stress, people respond by leaving earlier and/or staying longer in migration, by sending additional household members in migration or by receiving additional financial support from migrant family members. Today, temporary migration from rural areas in West Africa is a common activity for men, and increasingly also for women, and takes place irrespective of the quality of the yields. Encouraged by the seasonality of rainfall and a lack of local employment opportunities, migration is, for many farmers, a normal complementary activity to agriculture during the dry season. As such, migration is not only an important means to diversify income in order to cope with acute and future stress, but also constitutes an opportunity to accumulate financial resources and to increase the migrant's and the household's economic well-being.

Most households in rural areas today have both members who migrate for a longer period of time, mostly to work in urban areas, as well as members who stay in the rural area or only migrate during the dry season then returning for the harvest. While the latter group continues farming, the first group pursues other economic activities. The migration of entire households, however, is rare, since people usually are strongly attached to their land. Although the migration of one or several household members is, in most cases, crucial to support the household's income, this financial support is often not the main motive for leaving the village.

The seasonality of rainfall and the harsh environmental conditions in the West African Sahel certainly shape migration patterns. Although the migration motives are manifold, the public discourse tends to label Sahelian migrants as *environmental migrants*. The term *environmental migrant*, however, implies that environmental factors are the main determinants for people's migration. Moreover, most definitions, such as the often-cited IOM working definition of an *environmental migrant*, only refer to changes in the environment as a driver of migration. If, however, environmental conditions do not worsen but become increasingly unfavourable due to social changes and economic development, people will not fall under the definition. This is because the need for more money often results not from a worsening of environmental conditions, but actually from an improvement of living conditions or a higher demand for more cash, difficult to attain through agriculture alone. Yields may no longer correspond to the increasing demands for money and the aspirations for a better life, although environmental conditions may remain the same or even improve slightly. People who migrate in search for better employment opportunities are thus difficult to classify as *environmental migrants*.

Development and social transformation as an antidote to climate change

The common view among researchers and policy makers suggests that climate change will cause increased migration in the future. Nevertheless, the findings of this research suggest that development and social changes may reduce the impact of environmental stress on people's livelihoods and migration, despite worsening climate conditions. Why is this?

The success of migrants leads to development in the villages, improvements in income for the migrants and their families, but also to changing lifestyles and diminishing traditional social norms in the rural areas. It encourages migration because people want to have access and enjoy the same goods and lifestyle as their siblings, neighbours and peers, often only possible through migration. Limited employment opportunities in the rural areas outside of the agricultural sector make it difficult for those who prefer to stay in the village, but do not want to work in agriculture. Many young people from the rural areas, however, prefer to migrate because they consider life in the village boring and agriculture hard work. They leave the rural areas and the agricultural sector for better opportunities and more reliable and profitable employment in the urban areas, often inspired by the wish for economic independence and greater autonomy from the parents and village, by the desire for consumer goods, and by sheer curiosity.

As young people attain higher levels of education, this further fuels migration to urban areas. Most young people from the rural areas are better educated than their parents and do not want to pursue farming as a lifestyle. With a secondary level of education or higher, they are usually less dependent on agriculture and less vulnerable to environmental stress and have better access to well-paid employment. The highly educated rarely migrate for environmental reasons, instead for better opportunities for education or employment to improve their life prospects. Education levels have increased in both countries over the last decades and are likely to continue in the future. Considering social transformation processes, such as increasing education, urbanisation and changes in lifestyle, it is highly probable that young people will continue to leave the rural areas and discontinue working in (small-scale) agriculture. Development and social transformation processes may have a stronger impact on migration behaviour in the region than environmental stress while concurrently mitigating the impact of climate stressors on migration, despite worsening climate conditions.

Capabilities and aspirations as determinants of migration

In the West African Sahel, households usually benefit from the migration of their members. Thus, research mainly regards migration from areas affected by environmental change as a household adaptation strategy in response to households needs. However, migration is not always a household decision. Quite the contrary, the decision to migrate does not always match the will of the head of the household nor is it in the best interest of the household as a whole. Young migrants often do not even inform other household members about their plans to migrate. At a young age, migration is mainly a voluntary decision driven by individual aspirations and the need and/or expectation to contribute to the household's income.

Not everybody can freely decide whether to migrate or not: some need to migrate while others have to stay. In general, social norms restrict people's capabilities to decide over migration more than environmental stressors. Young men in the region are often expected to migrate and contribute to the household's income and thus may not be able to choose staying as an option. In contrast, women often face constraints with respect to migration. Married women need the permission of their husbands to migrate and the migration of young women is not desired and often prohibited, particularly in rural Mali. The need to migrate due to a lack of financial means seems to have become a socially accepted reason and excuse for young women from Mali to justify their migration even though their individual motive may differ from this reason.

If people have the capability to choose freely between migrating and staying, usually their aspirations and preferences determine the decision. Some people prefer to stay for reasons such as being close to their family, liking the calmness of the rural area or being attached to land and agriculture. Others decide to migrate for an assortment of reasons, such as economic gains, becoming successful, curiosity, a "modern" urban lifestyle or better educational and professional prospectives. A preference for migration is more likely if it is a desirable activity in the community or the peer group.

People who lack the capability to choose freely between migrating and staying are certainly disadvantaged at a personal level because they are less likely to lead lives they value and often highly depend on other household members. It is thus important to analyse people's capabilities and preferences to stay and to migrate in order to distinguish if people want or need to migrate or to stay, and for what reasons, in order to implement effective policy measures.

Recommendations for policy makers

In October 2016, the German Chancellor, Angela Merkel, chose Mali as one destination of her journey to three African countries. One of her goals: impeding a conceivable mass migration of young Africans to Europe. In light of the many refugees from Syria and other crisis countries coming to Germany in summer 2015, the prospect of African migrants entering Europe had suddenly become a realistic scenario. During her journey, Merkel offered to increase the amount of development aid from Germany to Mali and Niger in order to fight causes of flight and migration, particularly of young people. It was the first official visit of a German head of government to Mali, illustrating the importance attached to the subject. Although most people from rural Mali, Niger and other countries of the Sahel may still be too poor to pay for the dangerous journey across the Mediterranean, they are important transit countries.

People in West Africa are highly mobile and have a culture of mobility. Policy measures and development projects will (and should) therefore not stop people from moving, but reduce the need to move. Most people, however, move within their country or within the West African sub-region. Young people are usually aware of the risks of crossing the Sahara desert and the Mediterranean Sea and prefer to stay in the region, near families and friends, as long as the conditions allow for a decent life. Climate change and other environmental stressors are unlikely to be the main drivers of migration beyond the continent, because environmental migration takes place primarily in a short distance. Instead, the success of previous migrants and the dependence of the household on the migrant's financial support has not only changed people's aspirations for a better future but also increased the pressure on young people to improve the economic situation of the household.

Young Africans will not and cannot accept their fate to rest without opportunities on the African continent. If there are no good future prospects in their home countries or in the sub-region, young people will try to search for opportunities elsewhere and be ready to leave the continent despite the costs and risks. In Senegal, the level of development is much higher than in Mali with Senegal being one of the most developed countries in the region. Among the Senegalese, migration to Europe is more likely due to lesser opportunities in the less developed neighbouring countries and because people have the financial means and stronger social networks due to earlier international migration experience. In Mali, the precarious security situation and political instability during the last few years may have contributed to worsening economic opportunities and future prospects for young people. Moreover, young men may be easy targets for religious extremists and terrorists, active in Northern Mali. Increasing radicalisation among young people may then contribute to a further destabilisation of the country and the region and in turn will cause even more migration and flight.

Fostering people's opportunities in the region requires policies and interventions in several areas of concern and on different levels. Based on this book's findings, this includes two main strategies: a) improving the conditions in the rural areas for those who need or want to stay; and b) facilitating migration and improving the conditions in the destinations for those who want or have to migrate. The different strategies will tackle the needs of different types of migrants identified in the West African Sahel (see Chapter 8).

a)   Strategies to improve the conditions in the rural areas and mitigate the impact of climate change and environmental stressors for those who want or need to stay:

   i)   Improving infrastructure and services in order to create local employment and to make rural life more attractive for young people

Promoting rural development and local employment is one of the most urgent and probably most effective actions to reduce the necessity to migrate from the rural areas. Prerequisites for investments in income-generating activities and job creation are good and reliable infrastructure and services, both widely absent in the rural areas of Mali and Senegal. Electricity and running water supply are still rare and unreliable, if existent. Health and education infrastructure are poor at the community level and often even in the nearby towns. The quality of streets and the transportation infrastructure are poor with many communities experiencing access difficulties year round, particularly during the rainy season. Mobile phone networks are poor with little-to-no signal in many communities and internet is rarely accessible, and if so, it is unreliable and expensive.

This basic infrastructure is a precondition to draw investors into the rural areas and to enable people to run their own businesses. A better local infrastructure improves the opportunities for the rural population and makes life in the rural areas more pleasant and attractive for young people, particularly those who aspire to access certain goods, fashion, mobile phones, media, internet etc. Young people would like to be more connected to the global world, but are often unable to do so from their rural areas. The better the alternative local income opportunities, the lower the impact of environmental stress on people's livelihood. People may migrate despite local employment opportunities if economic incentives are higher or opportunities are better elsewhere, but the decision to migrate would be one of free choice. Improved infrastructures and services in the rural areas will benefit almost all types of migrants, but particularly the *Trapped*, the *Deprived*, the *Supplementers* and the *Transformers*, thus those who need to stay or those who would stay if there were better local employment opportunities.

ii) Providing insurance to compensate for losses in yields in the case of extreme weather events and ensuring access to investment capital

Many people are still highly dependent on the natural environment. They are usually the poorest people in the region with little opportunities outside of the agricultural sector and no or little support from migrant family members. Policies or interventions can be most effective by considering local differences with respect to livelihood stressors. While the response to acute environmental shocks, such as crop pests requires rapid action, the issue of lacking access to land as a consequence of population growth requires longer-term policy responses. Insurance that aims to compensate for losses in the event of major environmental shocks can reduce farmers' vulnerability to environmental stress. However, environmental change is often not the problem itself, but it has effects on economic exchange conditions, such as changes in relative prices that can lead to an economic emergency and/or famine. Offering people access to investment capital could enable them to invest in farming and livestock in order to reduce their vulnerability to external shocks. These measures will primarily favour the *Supplementers* and the *Deprived* migrants and reduce their need to migrate in order to ensure their livelihoods.

iii) Improving access to higher education

People with a secondary or higher level of formal education are less dependent on the natural environment and thus less vulnerable to environmental stress because they have better prospects for well-paid employment. Providing access to a good quality formal education, particularly to higher education at the secondary and tertiary level, requires an adequate education infrastructure and qualified teachers. Qualified teachers, however, are very unlikely to come and stay in the rural areas if no good infrastructure is present. Raising awareness among parents on the positive impact of education on children's future professional opportunities and providing financial aid for those who cannot afford to pay for learning materials can be supportive activities. The parents' positive attitude towards education is crucial in order to avoid that they oblige their children to work on the fields and force girls to get married at a young age, instead of letting them attend school. Improved access to higher education will benefit all types of migrants.

b) Strategies to facilitate migration within the country, within West Africa, and to Europe by improving the conditions in the destinations for those who want or have to migrate:

   i) Facilitating migration within the country: support for employment and accommodation

People who need to migrate due to environmental reasons do not fall under the legal protection affiliated with the refugee status because the UNHCR refugee convention only recognises those as refugees who have been forced to flee his or her country because of persecution, war or violence. Information centres and/or contact points for migrants in rural and urban areas could facilitate the search for employment and accommodation for those who do not have social networks and little financial means and reduce their risk of being a crime victim. Facilitating people's migration within the country and the sub-region would be an effective activity to support their ability to cope with and adapt to environmental stress, potentially preventing future displacement. Migration usually has a positive impact on development in the home community due to migrants' remittances and due to the transfer of valuable knowledge and skills to their rural areas upon return. Support for employment and accommodation would facilitate migration for all types of migrants, but particularly for those who do not have family support in the urban areas.

   ii) Improving infrastructure and employment opportunities in urban areas

In the West African Sahel, rural exodus and urbanisation will increase in the future, similarly to other parts of the world, irrespective of whether climate conditions worsen or not. Cities such as Abidjan, Bamako or Dakar have grown rapidly over the last decade while basic infrastructure has not expanded at the same pace. Interventions by policy makers need to improve urban infrastructure and services in order to meet the needs of new inhabitants and allow for a decent standard of living. This includes access to electricity, clean water, sanitation, affordable housing, health and schooling facilities. African cities have a high economic potential, yet employment opportunities are often rare or under degrading conditions whether for unskilled labour or people with a university degree. Government failure, corruption and the lack of stability and security are major barriers to private sector investment and consequently causes of limited employment opportunities in the region. Improved infrastructure and employment opportunities in the urban areas will benefit all migrants.

iii) Promoting mobility within West Africa and facilitating regular migration to Europe

Mobility within West Africa is common and should be facilitated and promoted. The preconditions are good: ECOWAS (Economic Community of West African States) provides a legal basis of free movement within the region and many countries use French as common language and the FCFA as currency, which facilitate the movement in the sub-region. In practice, however, free movement is often restricted, particularly for poor people. Policy makers from West Africa and Europe should raise awareness about the risks of irregular migration to Europe and inform potential migrants about employment and education opportunities in neighbouring countries and legal options to migrate to Europe. This, however, requires facilitating regular migration for young Africans to other West African countries as well as expanding legal pathways to migrate to European countries. Facilitated international migration benefits all migrants but particularly favours the *Well-Educated*, the *Adventurous* and the *Ambitious*.

Both rural and urban development are important because they tackle the needs of different groups of people. The focus of research and development policies may however (have to) shift to urban development because most people will live and search for opportunities in urban areas in the near future. Climate change may accelerate urbanisation but is unlikely to cause mass migration to Europe because people who are most vulnerable to environmental stress will not have the financial means and/or social networks to migrate to destinations across the continent. Instead, population growth and lack of opportunities in the West African Sahel may constitute the biggest challenge in the future. In Mali and Senegal, the vast majority of the population is under 24 years old. These young people are longing for opportunities to realise a better future, be it in their home countries, the sub-region or beyond the continent.

Index

For Product Safety Concerns and Information please contact our EU
representative GPSR@taylorandfrancis.com
Taylor & Francis Verlag GmbH, Kaufingerstraße 24, 80331 München, Germany

www.ingramcontent.com/pod-product-compliance
Ingram Content Group UK Ltd.
Pitfield, Milton Keynes, MK11 3LW, UK
UKHW020946180425
457613UK00019B/553